Grenada

Isle of Spice

Third Edition

Norma Sinclair

D0897037

MACMILLAN
CARIBBEAN

Macmillan Education
Between Towns Road, Oxford OX4 3PP
A division of Macmillan Publishers Limited
Companies and representatives throughout the world

www.macmillan-caribbean.com

ISBN 0 333 96806 9

First published 1987
Reprinted 1988, 1990
Second Edition 1992
Reprinted 1994, 1995
Third Edition 2002

Cover design by Gary Fielder, AC Design
Cover photographs by Nick Gillard (front) and Michael Bourne (back)

Commissioned photographs by Roger Brathwaite

Printed in Malaysia

2006   2005   2004   2003   2002
10   9   8   7   6   5   4   3   2   1

Contents

Fair Isles, where Nature's beauty beggars Art!
Could Painter's brush on canvas e'er portray
Perfection – how Earth, Sea, Air, Sky, all play
Each one an integral harmonious part?

From *The Call of the Caribbean* by Dr L. M. Commissiong

Introduction to the Third Edition

Change is ever constant.

Fourteen years have passed since the first publication of this book. In that time we have seen an increase in the number of National Parks, the opening up of new nature trails, the erection of a National Stadium suitable for hosting international sporting events, the start of construction of a new hospital, an increase in airport and seaport traffic, increased hotel and guest house accommodation – the list is endless.

Additions have been made to the historical chapter and various small changes were made here and there as necessary.

The only things that can never change are the beauty of these islands and the warmth of the inhabitants. We will always open our arms to visitors and make them welcome.

Introduction

Never in my wildest dreams did I ever consider writing a book. After a lovely meal ending with coffee on the verandah, in congenial company, one reaches a state of euphoria when nothing seems too difficult to tackle. My good friend Jean Baptiste chose just such a moment to suggest the writing of this guidebook and I was happy to comply. It would have gone no further without the encouragement and assistance of my husband who helped with the editing.

Grenada has had a very colourful past, when the English and French were fighting each other – and the Caribs – to gain control of the island. I particularly enjoyed writing about our history, which was originally meant to cover about two pages in Chapter 1, but I got so carried away that it had to be made into a chapter on its own.

I have tried to make this book an interesting experience to open the minds of my fellow Grenadians and our visitors alike to the beauty that is all around us. If I have succeeded in presenting an enjoyable companion, it will have been well worth the effort.

Many friends gave willingly of their time and knowledge and I take this opportunity to thank them all. However, I would particularly like to mention Garth Southwell, Denis Noel, Sydney Law and Raymond Steele from the Department of Agriculture and Fisheries; Curt Strachan, Clerk of Parliament; Michael Forshaw and Dod Gormon for their knowledge of the marine world; Julian Rapier and Willie Redhead who never tired of answering my questions, and last but not least, Sir William Branch whose wide knowledge and experience on Grenada's estates was invaluable.

In the historical chapter and those on birds and animals, I relied heavily on the 1946 edition of the *Grenada Handbook and Directory*, together with works written by Father Raymund P. Devas, OP, MC, and Dr J. R. Groome. Again, I thank my husband for his patience and support and dedicate this book to him.

To Eddie, with love

Foreword to the Third Edition

Having been asked by the author Mrs Sinclair to write a Foreword to her updated *Grenada: Isle of Spice* third edition, I felt very honoured and pleasantly surprised since I was not familiar with the contents of the previous editions.

However, from reading the second edition of *Grenada: Isle of Spice,* there is no question in my mind that this book depicts with clarity the true impressions of the Isle of Spice. While reading *Grenada: Isle of Spice* one gets a clear and picturesque description of the history, culture and people.

Mrs Sinclair's contribution to Grenada, Carriacou and Petit Martinique cannot be underestimated. As a true patriot she has been consistent in her writing and her portrayal of this beautiful island.

For the prospective visitor **Grenada: Isle of Spice** is an excellent buy as you contemplate visiting our shores. To the many Grenadians who have not read this book I encourage you to get a copy.

Grenada: Isle of Spice is a book that reaches out and invites readers to journey with the author through the pages expecting a wonderful experience.

This book is well written and easy to read. Therefore I recommend this volume very highly to our readers.

Brenda Hood
Minister for Tourism, Civil Aviation, Social Security, Gender and Family Affairs

Foreword to the Second Edition

I felt extremely honoured to be asked by Mrs Norma Sinclair, author of *Grenada: Isle of Spice*, to write a foreword to her latest, updated edition. This important volume on Grenada brings together in clear and concise form the history, culture, social institutions, physical attributes and natural environment of this our beautiful *'Isle of Spice'*.

I am particularly proud and sincerely appreciative of Mrs Sinclair's significant contribution to our country Grenada, Carriacou and Petite Martinique. Her love, interest, commitment and involvement are very clearly reflected in the way she writes and the amount of research she must have done to put this lively documentary together. Not only is her work important and valuable to our many visitors, who I am sure will find the vivid descriptions absorbing, captivating and exerting a decided pull to come and see for themselves, but to all Grenadians, especially our youth, who desire a quick snapshot of our past and present, in a form that is readable and affordable.

I have no hesitation in recommending this important volume to our readers.

Joan Purcell
Minister for Tourism, Civil Aviation and Women's Affairs

Foreword

When Mrs Norma Sinclair asked me if I would write a Foreword to her 'Guidebook on Grenada' as she described it to me, I readily agreed to do so as Chairman of the Grenada Tourist Board, expecting another of the usual commercial publications intended for the quick and ready reference of the visitor to Grenada.

However, as I read through the draft pages of this volume I quickly realised that this was more than a routine guidebook. It is one of the most comprehensive publications which provides its readers with factual information on all aspects of life in the State of Grenada, Carriacou and Petit Martinique. It opens the window on the historical and cultural heritage of our people; on the crops we grow, some of which like the spices, are truly 'native' to Grenada – hence the title *Grenada: Isle of Spice*; on the way we cook and the foods we eat; on the games we play and the numerous ways we enjoy ourselves. The description of the various parts of our country is so vivid that one can create in his or her mind a picture of the area which would not be far from the real thing and which would cause no disappointment to the visitor to our shores.

It will not be too difficult for the readers of this publication to get the 'feel' of our country, to want to come and enjoy the warmth and friendliness of our people, and to have the desire to experience and participate in our cultural and recreational activities in an atmosphere of 'a home away from home'.

It is with a feeling of pride and pleasure that I commend *Grenada: Isle of Spice* by Norma Sinclair to our readers.

Sir John A. Watts

Former Chairman, Grenada Tourist Board.

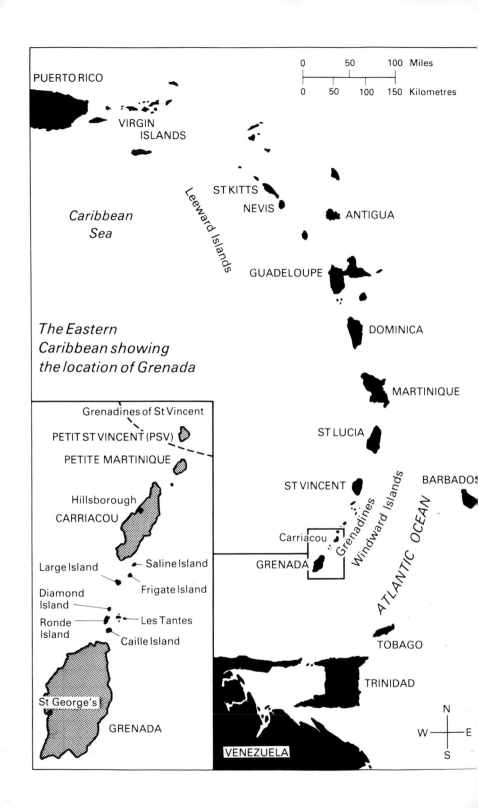

PUERTO RICO

VIRGIN
ISLANDS

Caribbean
Sea

Leeward Islands

ST KITTS
NEVIS
ANTIGUA

GUADELOUPE

The Eastern
Caribbean showing
the location of Grenada

DOMINICA

MARTINIQUE

ST LUCIA

0   50   100 Miles
0   50   100   150 Kilometres

Grenadines of St Vincent
PETIT ST VINCENT (PSV)
PETITE MARTINIQUE

Hillsborough
CARRIACOU

Large Island ———— Saline Island

Diamond
Island
Ronde
Island ——— Les Tantes
Caille Island
Frigate Island

St George's

GRENADA

ST VINCENT

BARBADOS

Carriacou

GRENADA

Grenadines

Windward Islands

ATLANTIC OCEAN

TOBAGO

TRINIDAD

N
W — E
S

VENEZUELA

| 1 |
Something about the island

Only superlatives can describe this island. It is truly the most beautiful in a chain of lovely islands that stretch in a graceful curve between the continents of North and South America. The line of latitude 12° North of the equator passes through the southern end of the island, and we are positioned about 61° 40′ West longitude. Grenada is the furthest south in the group of islands comprising the Lesser Antilles, and one of the four known as the Windward Islands. St Vincent, St Lucia and Dominica are the other three. Between St Vincent and Grenada, several small islands stretch along a submarine ridge like a chain of emeralds in a sea of sapphire. From the air the view is spectacular. Of these islands, Carriacou and Petite Martinique are included in the State of Grenada, the other islands being governed by St Vincent.

Trinidad is about 90 miles (145 km) south of us and St Vincent about 70 miles (113 km) to the north-north-east.

A long view of the beautiful Grand Anse Beach (ROGER BRATHWAITE)

1

Physical

With our island dependencies, we boast an area of 133 square miles (344 sq km). A range of hills runs basically north to south through the centre of the island of Grenada, the highest of which, Mt St Catherine in the northern half of the island, reaches a height of 2756 feet (841 metres) above sea level. There are numerous streams (which we call rivers) and some mineral springs. Four crater lakes bear testimony to the island's volcanic origin. The hills and valleys that were forced up and pressed down in that era of violent upheaval contribute to the breathtaking beauty that is all around us. The rich volcanic soil provides our lush vegetation. Some gardeners claim that any seed will grow with the minimum of attention.

In the unbelievably clear seas around us, coral formations have built up over a millennium or more, and provide us with a fabulous underwater display of living things that boggles the imagination. Most beaches are of white coral sand; some are of a softer, almost silky sand of black volcanic origin. One would think that this in itself describes an island paradise. We have been further blessed. There are no poisonous snakes or insects and no dangerous animals, and our volcanoes are all extinct. What more could anyone ask for?

The north-east trade winds keep the island refreshingly cool most of the year, and we enjoy an average annual shade temperature of 85°F (30°C), rising as high as 95°F (35°C) in the daytime during the hot months of August to November. In the cooler months of December to March, the temperature may drop at night in the mountainous areas as low as 65°F (18°C).

There are two seasons: the dry season lasts from January to May, when the hills get brown from the lack of sufficient rainfall and the rivers are very low – some a mere trickle. This is the time when plants and flowers are collected for the beautiful dried flower arrangements that are to be seen in so many of our hotels. Even in these months we experience a certain amount of light rainfall which is known locally as 'dry season rain'. In the wet season, from June to December, we can expect much heavier showers, though they seldom last for more than an hour at a time, leaving the land with a fresh, clean smell. The rivers fill quickly and this is the time to enjoy a river bathe. There is nothing harmful in our rivers and the visitor will find the waters cool and refreshing. At this time, the land seems to turn from brown to green almost overnight.

A white sandy beach at Sauteurs *opposite* (ROGER BRATHWAITE)

As can be expected, the highest rainfall occurs in the hilly areas, which record an average annual rainfall of about 160 inches (4 metres). The coastal areas average about 50 inches (1.3 metres) per year, with the southern end of the island being the most arid. This area is not very good for agriculture but, with its magnificent beaches, it is perfect for our visitors who are looking for just such a spot in which to enjoy the sunshine and to swim in the calm, clear waters of the Caribbean Sea.

The islands of the Grenadines are normally drier and on Carriacou the average annual rainfall is about 45 inches (1.1 metres).

Over the years we have experienced heavy thunderstorms, but there has been only one hurricane in the known history of the island – Janet – which occurred in September, 1955. We do not expect a repeat visit for another five hundred years or so.

Our government

Grenada is a fully independent country. Its head of state is Her Majesty the Queen, Elizabeth II, Head of the Commonwealth, who is

The Houses of Parliament in St George's (SINCLAIR)

4

represented on the island by a Governor General. The government of Grenada is democratically elected. Members of the Cabinet are responsible for executing, enforcing and administering the laws passed in Parliament. The Prime Minister, as head of government, presides over the Cabinet.

The Houses of Parliament are divided into two. The lower house, or House of Representatives, has fifteen elected members. The Speaker may be chosen from the members, or from persons who are not members in which case he or she (the Speaker) becomes the sixteenth member of the House. The upper house or the Senate, consists of thirteen members, all appointed by the Governor General; seven on the advice of the Prime Minister, three on the advice of the Leader of the Opposition and three on the advice of the Prime Minister after consultation with organisations which he or she considers the senators should be selected to represent. The President of the Senate is elected from among the senators.

We have our own national anthem, flag and coat of arms with the motto: 'Ever conscious of God we aspire, build and advance as one people'.

Grenada is a member of the Commonwealth as well as many international organisations including the United Nations, the Organisation of American States, the Caribbean Community and the Organisation of Eastern Caribbean States.

Our economy

There has been a slow but steady growth in our economy over the past few years. Tourism and agriculture form the basis of this trend. There has also been marked improvement in the areas of manufacturing and of building construction. It is felt however, that the building industry has reached its peak and will show a decline in future years. The government is committed to economic diversification with emphasis being placed on development of the service sector. Tourism will play a vital role in any future economic strategy and new areas already considered are offshore financial services and markets for exotic flowers and fruit. There is also a thriving fishing industry.

Small cottage industries are encouraged. Leather shoes and bags are produced locally, as well as woven mats and baskets in bamboo or cane. Jams, jellies, sweets and beverages are made from native fruit. A small candle making factory supplies the local market and batik lovers can choose interesting and unique designs fashioned and produced locally.

Education

Grenada is one of the few islands of the English-speaking Caribbean to have a well-established system of education. This begins with early childhood education at the age of $2\frac{1}{2}$ and carries through to the secondary school level up to age 19. Many of the schools here were founded by church groups. Now there is an arrangement between Church and State for dual control of schools. All schools come under the general control of the Ministry of Education. School leaving examinations at the High School level are set by the Caribbean Examinations Council (CXC) and/or Cambridge Board of Education in the UK. The CXC serves sixteen Caribbean territories. Their exams are equivalent to GCSE standard. The University of the West Indies, the St George's University as well as several institutions for higher education further afield, recognise these qualifications.

The T. A. Marryshow Community College provides tertiary level education to the standard of Cambridge 'A' level as well as associate degrees and Caribbean Advanced Proficiency Exams (CAPE). Technical and vocational education for young adults is also undertaken at this college. Additionally, there is a division for teacher education that trains teachers for the primary school system.

There is a school of continuing studies financed by the University of the West Indies.

The St George's University is an American administered institution which was founded in 1976 as a school of medicine. It has expanded into healthcare education by instituting graduate and undergraduate programmes. In 1996 it was granted a charter for its School of Arts and Sciences and its School of Graduate Studies. All programmes are conducted in English.

In addition to the formal school system there is a skills training institution in St Andrew's as well as the New Life Organisation (commonly referred to as NEWLO) in the parish of St John.

St George's is blessed with a natural harbour *opposite* (ROGER BRATHWAITE)

Disabled children are given special instruction at the Grenada School for Special Education in the parish of St George and at the St Andrew's School for Special Education in the north of the island. There is also a school for deaf children.

Employment

A large percentage of our young people find it difficult to obtain gainful employment. There is still a reluctance to go into agriculture which is an important factor in retaining the stability of the island's economy.

Government has embarked on a number of projects. A new sports stadium has been built in Grenada, a mini stadium in Carriacou and a new ministerial complex in St George's. There is a massive roads reconstruction project in progress. Facilities at St George's port have been enlarged. Work continues on the reconstruction of the General Hospital in the nation's capital as well as the expansion of the fish market. Plans are on stream for the construction of a new cruise ship terminal at St George's as well as several other projects around the island, all of which will provide much needed employment.

Efforts are being made by the government and the private sector to steer youth into self-employment and small business enterprises.

Work permits are not easily obtained by non-Grenadians wishing to reside and work here unless it is in a specialised field not already available on the island.

Communications

Cable & Wireless Grenada Ltd, a subsidiary of the worldwide communications group, operates a fully automatic nine-exchange dial system throughout Grenada, Carriacou and Petite Martinique. Direct dialling is possible to the vast majority of countries in the world. The company also offers telex, facsimile, Internet, credit card calling and other telecommunication services. Their offices on the Carenage in St George's and at Hillsborough in Carriacou are open Monday to Friday from 7.30 a.m. to 6.00 p.m. On Saturdays they open from 7.30 a.m. to 1.00 p.m. and on Sundays from 10.00 a.m. to 12.00 noon. Their Carriacou office does not open on Sundays and public holidays. Public cardphones are available throughout the islands. There is also a mobile service, a paging service and Cable & Wireless voicemail.

Looking towards Fort George *opposite* (SINCLAIR)

Overseas calls can be made from the Calling Centre at their main office on the Carenage. In this way we cater for the most sophisticated and the busiest of executives who can escape from it all, knowing full well that contact with the outside world is but a phone call away.

The Grenada Postal Corporation in St George's was registered as a statutory body in January 1998 to take over the operation of the government-run General Post Office. There are 52 postal stations and six sub-offices throughout the state. The postal services are open Monday to Friday 8.00 a.m. to 4.00 p.m. Only stamps can be purchased between 11.45 and 1.00 p.m. as all other sections are closed for lunch. Express mail services are available to the United States and all Caribbean countries. Registration facilities have been extended to the post offices in Grand Anse and Brizan. Private letter boxes are available at their St George's office and at Grand Anse.

The corporation is closed at weekends.

Electricity

The Grenada Electricity Services Ltd supplies the island with electricity at a rating of 220/240 volts, 50 cycles AC.

Water

The National Water and Sewerage Authority (NAWASA) was established in 1991. Three independent water supply systems are operated in Grenada and these provide us with good quality, treated water which is collected from our many rivers and streams.

Some hotels in the south of the island have also installed de-salination plants to help cater for the influx of visitors during our summer festivities and for the winter months December/April each year.

Population

The population is an intermixture of the numerous races that settled on the island in the past four hundred years and is predominantly of African origin. By the mid-1970s it was estimated that the population had risen to 110,000 but with the subsequent years of political uncertainty, a mass exodus diminished the numbers to about 89,000 according to a 1981 census. By 1991 this figure had risen to 95,597 and the latest estimated figure (in the year 2000) is 101,377.

Health care

The General Hospital in St George's is well equipped with private, maternity and public wards, a casualty and outpatients' department, X-ray facilities, a laboratory, operating theatres and an eye clinic, all with well-trained staff.

This institution is presently undergoing some major reconstruction and the completion of phase one is scheduled for early 2001. On final completion, the hospital will be a 245-bed facility.

Recently, the St George's University opted to use it as a teaching hospital for their medical students, and all facilities will be upgraded to meet this requirement.

Additionally, there is a district hospital in the parish of St Andrew and one in Carriacou, together with health centres and visiting stations throughout the islands.

There are also two private medical facilities in St George's offering an extensive range of health care services, all with well-qualified staff.

Dental facilities are easily available from well-trained and experienced dentists.

A number of retirement homes are based around the main island and through a programme known as ECHO (Extended Care for Hope and Optimism), older citizens who find it difficult to manage by themselves can still remain in their homes and get trained help to assist with cleaning and cooking on a regular basis.

Many private doctors and nurses are on call, and there are several nursing homes and homes for the elderly around the island as well as in Carriacou.

Our idiosyncrasies

Although English is the spoken language, the Gallic influence can still be seen in our inclination to gesticulate while speaking, and in some expressions used, the most common being one of indignation, 'Well yes, oui!' 'Bun Jay' (Bon Dieu) is another popular expression. Patois is no longer so commonly spoken but there is still a slight confusion of syntax even though the meaning is quite clear. 'Bring it come!' 'Look me here' and 'Rain drizzling!' are easily understood.

This story should give the visitor an idea of our relaxed approach:

Two young men, a stranger and a local, were admiring a very attractive young lady being escorted by a local hotelier.
Said the local, 'She's a Dey Wid!'
'What do you mean?' asked his friend.
'They not married, she only dey wid' he.'
Which meant that she was living with him (there with him).

A number of superstitions remain, culled from our rich and varied heritage. With the passage of time our pronunciation of some words differs slightly, but the meaning is the same:

The Ligaroo (loup-garou; English: werewolf) sheds and hides his skin, then changes into a ball of fire and pursues his victims to bite them and suck their blood. The only way to catch him is to find his skin and sprinkle salt on it. That will give him an uncontrollable itch when he puts it back on, thus he is easily identified.

Lajabless (la diablesse) is a demon woman with a beautiful body. She is often seen under a huge silk cotton tree, wearing a large floppy hat to hide her face, which is a skull, and long skirts to hide her feet, one of which is cloven. Her male victims are enticed to lonely spots, usually near a precipice. When she lifts her hat, they are either driven insane, or end their lives by jumping over the precipice.

Obeah is a type of witchcraft originating in Africa, which is still practised in these islands.

Some people are known by two completely different names. A child may be baptised 'Peter Jones' but, for fear that the spirits might get to know his real name, he might be known to his friends and family as 'Raphael Smith'. This is his 'home' name. Many of these children are born to unwed mothers and it is not unusual for them to use their father's surname. This is confusing, but acceptable.

| 2 |
Points of historical interest

Grenada was 'discovered' a long time before Christopher Columbus sighted the island on this third voyage to the New World in 1498.

It is believed that aeons ago the sea was about 300 feet lower than it is at the present day, so that much more land was visible in this region. The islands of the Grenadines, from Bequia to Grenada, were all one area of land. The South American continent was nearer too, with just about 28 miles of sea separating our land area from the mainland. Consequently, it is easy to see how early settlers could have travelled from the mainland up through the islands.

The first human inhabitants that can be traced were a very primitive race called the Siboneys. This was the name given them by the Arawaks who met them here. The name means 'stone people'.

Cobblestones and steps lead from the Bay Town to Church Street (SINCLAIR)

The Arawaks were the next race to settle here. They appear to have been a simple, peaceful people, though more advanced than the Siboneys. Their staple foods were fish and cassava which they cultivated and processed into a type of bread. Their petroglyphs can still be seen on rocks in certain parts of the island.

Some time later, a more warlike race of Amerindians arrived in their canoes. They raided and ransacked the peaceful Arawak settlements, killed the men and kept the women as their slaves. They were a fierce, proud people – a nomadic race known among themselves as the 'Callinagos'. Their new island home they named 'Camerhogne'.

These Indians sailed freely between the islands and were known to come to each other's assistance in times of need. When the Europeans arrived, they chose the name of Carib for this warlike race. The entire area became known as the Caribees, now called the Caribbean.

The Caribs lived in villages and, apart from the crops that they grew, they lived on fruit, fish, shellfish, game and small birds. When the Europeans arrived, they would enjoy a feast of European flesh on occasion to satisfy their cannibalistic instincts. It seems that the French were considered the most tasty!

This island went through several changes of name. Columbus called her 'Concepción'. 'Mayo' was the name chosen by Amerigo Vespucci and his map-makers. 'Granada' appeared in earlier maps of the sixteenth century when theoretically we were a Spanish island although no Spaniards ever settled on these shores. The fierce Caribs were able to keep the island to themselves for about 150 years after that first sighting. Then in 1609 a company of London merchants attempted the first settlement of the island. By the end of that year, the remaining few returned to Britain.

The French then tried in 1638 but that attempt was also crushed by the Caribs. Eventually, in 1650, M. du Parquet, who with M. Houel had purchased Martinique, St Lucia and Grenada from the Company of the Isles of America, brought 299 adventurers to this island. He was well known to the Caribs here through their frequent trips to Martinique, and in exchange for some quantities of cloth, hatchets, knives, glass beads and two bottles of *eau-de-vie* (brandy), he purchased the whole island from the Carib Chief, save and except their houses and the land that they cultivated. 'Granada' now became 'La Grenade'. Within a few months, hostilities opened between the

14

The buildings in St George's rise theatrically up the surrounding ridges
(SINCLAIR)

settlers and the Caribs. Du Parquet sent reinforcements from Martinique, the Caribs received reinforcements from Dominica and St Vincent, and the fighting began in earnest. The Caribs, even with their poisoned arrows, were no match for the French firearms and the war culminated in the slaughter of Carib warriors save about forty who, rather than surrender, ran down a hillside at the north end of the island and threw themselves over a precipice on to the rocks in the angry waters below, perishing to a man. This bluff became known as 'Le Morne des Sauteurs' (Leapers' Hill) and to this day the town that grew up in that area is known as Sauteurs (pronounced So-tairs).

In 1654 after atrocities had been committed against them in some of the islands to the north, there was a general uprising of all the Caribs and swiftly, from one island to the next, the message was passed on: 'To every white man, Death.' In Grenada, this caused the final defeat and complete massacre of the remaining Carib population and the destruction of their villages and crops.

M. du Parquet sold the island in 1657 to the Comte de Cerillac who, in turn, sold it to the French West India Company in 1665. In

1674 with the dissolution of that company, Grenada came directly under the dominion of the French Crown. The original town called Port Louis was removed from a strip of land in the area of the lagoon to its present site in 1705. The new town became known as Fort Royal, probably after the erection of the protecting fort in the following year. Over a period of about 150 years, that original strip of land gradually submerged and disappeared altogether. Later a channel was cut so that yachts could enter this safe harbour which is considered an ideal shelter from storms.

In March 1762, after capturing the islands of Guadeloupe, Martinique and St Lucia, a British fleet sailed for Grenada, and the island capitulated without one shot being fired. From then, the island was known to the British as Grenada (pronounced Gre-nay-dah). The town was renamed St George's and the citadel at the entrance to the harbour became Fort George.

It is interesting to note that, by the Treaty of Paris signed the following year – 10th February 1763 – Grenada remained in the hands of the British whereas St Lucia and Martinique were handed back to the French in return for all the French possessions in Canada!

A disastrous fire destroyed St George's in 1771 and again in 1775. It was after this that many of the beautiful old Georgian brick buildings were constructed with their fish-scale-type clay-tiled roofs. The bricks and tiles were brought over as ballast on the ships sailing from Europe to collect our sugar and other produce in the seventeenth and eighteenth centuries.

In early 1779 the powerful British fleet in these islands was forced to convoy a large fleet of merchant vessels on their way to Great Britain. The French seized the opportunity to capture St Vincent. Then, as they received reinforcements, they set out to attack Barbados, but the elements were against them. The winds were so strong that they abandoned this idea and sailed instead for Grenada. The battle lasted about two days and the French were again in possession of the island. It was at this time that the construction of a fort at Richmond Hill was commenced. This was completed by the British who resumed possession when, by the Treaty of Versailles in 1783, Grenada was again ceded to Great Britain.

The British in the island began by demanding the use of the French Roman Catholic churches and lands; when permission was refused, they were seized by the government and handed over to the Protestant Church and the Crown. This naturally caused a great deal

16

At River Antoine Estate, sugar cane is still crushed in the old-fashioned way via a water wheel (ROGER BRATHWAITE)

of dissatisfaction among the French planters and free coloureds who were mostly of French Catholic extraction.

In 1790 a number of French inhabitants, including Julien Fédon, a coloured landowner, made a public profession of their loyalty to Great Britain and asked the government for protection against certain 'base and designing' Frenchmen who had come from Martinique to disturb the peace. This was at the start of the Revolution in France (1789) and unrest was beginning to spread among the islands. The Governor, Ninian Home, and his government made no attempt to assist, and did not try to protect the inhabitants in any way from the propaganda being spread by the new arrivals. As if this were not enough, the government apparently strove to alienate the Catholic population still further. They were debarred from taking any part in the affairs of the colony, a privilege which they had enjoyed during the previous occupation by the British. All this dissatisfaction culminated in the savage rebellion led by Julien Fédon in March 1795 in which he hoped, with aid from Guadeloupe, to make Grenada a part of the new French Republic and abolish slavery. It took about fifteen months and the loss of many lives, including that of the

17

Governor and several other British subjects who were cruelly executed, before this rebellion was quelled. Fédon himself escaped but all the other leaders were captured and killed. Then began an era of uneasy truce between the British and the remaining French settlers on the island.

Recovery was slow as immense damage had been done island-wide to buildings and crops.

With the complete emancipation of slaves in 1838 the plantations again suffered a serious setback as many of the ex-slaves were reluctant to continue working on the estates. They chose to take up trades or to settle or squat on a small portion of Crown lands which they cultivated for themselves and their families. With money realised from the sale of charcoal and surplus garden produce, their lives were reasonably comfortable.

In an effort to save the sugar industry, 164 labourers were imported from Malta in 1839. By 1844, after some severe droughts and a fall in sugar prices, several estates had been abandoned or were only partially cultivated. In 1846/47, Portuguese came from Madeira and in 1849, liberated slaves from Africa. Estate production began to show some improvement.

East Indian immigration began in 1857. At this time, whale fishing (mostly by American whalers) furnished lucrative alternative employment to labouring on the estates. In this century too, some of the descendants of English settlers in Barbados found themselves without employment because of the change in the economy brought about by the emancipation of slaves. They were conveyed to other Caribbean islands by the established Church and those brought to Grenada formed a colony of their own on a hill named Mt Moritz just outside the capital. They were industrious and hardworking planters, and kept very much to themselves for nearly a century. In the 1970s a large number of the younger generation emigrated to Australia and the remaining youth are gradually being integrated into the wider Grenadian community.

The island was proclaimed a Crown Colony in 1877.

In 1881 Grenada was admitted into the Postal Union and the telephone exchange in St George's came into existence in 1891. Prior to this, there had been a small telephone link through the police stations all over the island which private citizens were allowed to use in cases of emergency.

In 1895 the island's first fire brigade was established.

By the late nineteenth century a number of primary and secondary schools had been built, and there was a coastal steamer service which brought the villages and the island of Carriacou in touch with St George's. Up to that time the roads had not been paved and horses, mules and donkeys were ridden and used to pull the carriages and carts.

About this time also the inhabitants began protesting to Britain against the Crown Colony system of government, which they thought unfair on account of their inability to participate fully in local affairs. Dr William Wells and later Mr W. Galway Donovan were strong contenders in this struggle against Britain.

So many estates had been abandoned that they were eventually sold out in small lots to the former labourers. A census taken in 1881 showed that out of 9000 adult males in the colony, no less than 3000 were owners of lots from one to fifty acres. By 1911 the number of small landowners had risen to 8349.

By the dawn of the twentieth century there was a full network of macadamised roads (about 400 miles altogether), a good water supply to the capital and to many of the other towns. A telephone network extended island-wide, and was linked to telegraph communication with the rest of the world.

Early in this century there was a large exodus of the population. The high prices paid for labour on the US Government operation on the Panama Canal attracted 1534 Grenadian labourers. Many Grenadians also emigrated to find work at the oil refineries in Curaçao and Aruba.

Standard Time, four hours earlier than Greenwich Mean Time, was adopted in Grenada, along with other West Indian colonies, from 1st July 1911.

The Grenadian Chronicle, a newspaper which had been in circulation since 1784, ceased publication in 1915. It had been the oldest newspaper in the western hemisphere, and the second oldest in the English speaking world, having been established even before *The Times* in London.

Motor cars began making an appearance, and by 1919 there were two hundred in addition to motor lorries. Presently there are approximately 17,600 vehicles on the road. This includes motor bicycles and heavy duty vehicles.

Protestations which began in the last century against the system of government were still being voiced, and Mr T. Albert Marryshow, a

19

young journalist, came to the forefront in this struggle. As a result of this, a more acceptable form of government was given to Grenada in 1924.

Electricity came first to the town of St George's in 1929 and gradually spread to other towns around the island. In 1939 an 850-foot long pier was opened in St George's and in 1943 a small airfield at Pearls in the north of the island came into operation.

One of the worst disasters in the island's known history was the loss of the schooner *Island Queen*. Two schooners left Grenada on 5th August 1944 full of holidaymakers bent on spending the long weekend in St Vincent. The *Island Queen*, with its 56 passengers and 11 crew, was never heard from again and the whole island mourned them. Everybody had either family or good friends on board, and there were weeks of uncertainty, hope and prayers before we became reconciled to the fact that we would never see our loved ones again.

In 1951 universal adult suffrage was established for all persons of twenty-one years and over. This year also marked the rise in power of Eric Gairy who entered the political arena. He was a Grenadian migrant worker who was deported from Aruba in 1949 for causing disturbances there. Mr Gairy fought for better wages and conditions for the farm workers and this was an era of strikes and much damage to property and the economy generally. His party swept the polls in 1951 and this flamboyant figure rode roughshod over the political scene for the next 28 years whether in or out of power. Although he managed to achieve a better standard of living for the poorer Grenadian workers, his governments were corrupt and wasteful, having complete disregard for the laws and regulations governing public finance in Grenada.

On 22nd September 1955 Grenada was hit by 'Janet', a severe hurricane. About 120 lives were lost and there was widespread damage to property. Our forests were almost completely denuded and most of our nutmeg and cocoa trees were destroyed. While trying to recover from this economic catastrophe, many of the estates began cultivating bananas as a stopgap while the nutmeg and cocoa trees were replanted. This saved the island from complete financial ruin, and bananas have become our third major export crop.

The West Indies was formed into a Federation in 1958, and Mr Marryshow became one of the senators. Unfortunately, his dream of a West Indian Nation lasted no more than four years, but he did

Samaritan Estate Great House, in the north of the island (MICHAEL BOURNE)

not live to see its demise, having died in October 1958. In the Caribbean Mr Marryshow is fondly known as 'The Father of Federation' – a well-deserved title. He fought hard for better conditions in these islands, and represented the town of St George's for a record 33 years of unbroken service.

Grenada became an Associated State of Great Britain in 1967, with the legislature gaining full control of Grenada's internal affairs, and Britain retaining responsibility for the island's defence and external affairs. Mr H. A. Blaize became the first Premier of this Associated State. Later that year, Mr Gairy's party again won the elections from the more moderate party headed by Mr Blaize.

In 1968 one of Grenada's most outstanding women, Dr Hilda Bynoe, a medical practitioner, married to a Trinidad born architect, was appointed the first native Governor of the State of Grenada, and became the first woman Governor of a Commonwealth country. Her Excellency was later awarded the accolade of Dame Commander of the Most Excellent Order of the British Empire. Dame Hilda and her husband now reside in Trinidad.

On 7th February 1974 the country was granted independence from Great Britain with provision in the constitution for persons of 18 years and over to vote. Mr Gairy became our first Prime Minister. This increased the power of this autocratic ruler which ended with his overthrow in 1979 in a coup which took place while he was away from the state. The New Jewel Movement (NJM) which organised the coup, was an amalgamation of dissenting groups that got together in 1973 to form a stronger opposition force. Their condemnation of Mr Gairy's rule caused their leaders to be mercilessly beaten on more than one occasion. After the coup, the People's Revolutionary Government (PRG) assumed control of the island's affairs.

The Constitution of 1974 was suspended and People's Laws were passed to legalise this government's actions. To allay the fears of the population, promises were made that, as soon as the country was more settled, constitutional government would be returned. Mr Maurice Bishop, the leader of the party, took over the premiership with the deputy leader, Mr Bernard Coard, being made Minister of Finance.

Slowly it began to dawn on the populace that the new government's ideology was firmly based on a Marxist system of government. The press was stifled and the prison became packed with political prisoners. No one dared to question any of the government's actions.

The young nation was saved from communist rule when dissension broke out between the party leaders. Mr Bishop was put under house arrest and subsequently executed by his own militia in October 1983. A four-day curfew was imposed on the entire nation, with the threat that anyone on the streets would be shot on sight. The 23rd October 1983 was the first Sunday in the history of Grenada that no church services were held.

At the request of our Governor General, Sir Paul Scoon through the Organisation of Eastern Caribbean States (OECS), OECS and American forces on 25 October 1983 overran the remaining communist element and installed an interim government. Mr Nicholas Brathwaite was appointed to head this government which prepared the country for general elections the following year, and then was dissolved.

The Deputy Prime Minister of the NJM government Mr Bernard Coard, his wife Mrs Phyllis Coard and 12 other party members were tried and found guilty of Mr Bishop's murder. They were sentenced to death. This sentence was later commuted to life imprisonment. Three other soldiers were sentenced to 30-year prison terms.

The constitution was gradually restored and elections were held a year later. The New National Party, an alliance of three political groups, won all but one of the fifteen seats in the House of Representatives and Carriacou-born H. A. Blaize was now chosen as Prime Minister of the State of Grenada (comprising the islands of Grenada, Carriacou and Petite Martinique).

On 26th October 1984 the new international airport at Point Salines in the south of the island was officially opened. Started by the PRG with much assistance from Cuba and other communist bloc countries, it was completed with the aid of Britain, Canada and the United States of America.

The alliance lasted for a very short time, with elected members resigning in protest against the manner in which certain issues were handled by the Prime Minister. In our newly restored democracy it was thought by many that Mr Blaize was stubborn, hard headed and somewhat dictatorial in his treatment of several important government matters.

Sir Eric Gairy returned to Grenada in 1984 from the United States of America where he had lived in voluntary exile since his overthrow in 1979.

In January 1989 at a party convention Mr Blaize was deposed from the leadership of the NNP and Dr Keith Mitchell, General Secretary of the party and the Minister for Communications and Works, was elected in his place. This led to a complete disruption within the party, culminating in the dismissal of Dr Mitchell from the Cabinet and eventually to the formation of a new party by Mr Blaize and a few stalwarts – The National Party (TNP).

Severe illness dogged his term in office which was also fraught with other difficulties. Opposition members in Parliament were pressing the Prime Minister to name a date for elections; Dr Mitchell threatened to call for a vote of 'no confidence' in the government, and Mr Blaize decided to prorogue Parliament. The civil servants then began agitating for salary increases which were promised in early December but not received, as the anticipated source of funding was no longer available. This news was delivered to the three unions representing the public workers just one day before the increases were to be paid. The unions were understandably very angry and their workers were ordered to strike until the money was paid. Millions of dollars in revenue were lost during this strike. The government eventually raised the necessary amount by the sale of

23

some of its shares in the local telephone company to Cable & Wireless. This sale did not go down at all well with members of the opposition or with the general public. Amidst this turmoil Mr Blaize passed away on 19th December 1989 just months before elections were due to be called. He has been the longest serving member of the legislature in the history of Grenada.

In March 1990 Grenadians again went to the polls with a choice of candidates from five parties. The National Democratic Congress emerged the winners of seven seats. They needed one more to command a slight majority in order to form the new government. It was necessary therefore for the NDC to join forces with another party, or to woo elected members from other parties into their fold.

Eventually the TNP candidate Mr Ben Jones, the leader of his party since the death of Mr Blaize, agreed to join forces with the NDC, and a GULP elected member defected from his party (whose leader was Sir Eric Gairy) and joined the new government.

Within weeks of the elections, Grenada suffered a severe setback when on 27th April 1990 the entire financial complex went on fire and all records were lost. Only the old brick walls remained standing to show where once the beautiful Georgian buildings graced our waterfront, housing the Ministry of Finance, the Government

Looking out to sea from St George's (SINCLAIR)

Treasury, tax departments, printery, statistical department and the Post Office. Assistance from the United Kingdom was requested to determine the origin of the fire and it was found that faulty electrical wiring had caused this massive damage. Our Minister for Finance estimated the loss at about EC$19m, but many of the records will be irreplaceable. Members of the private sector immediately came to the government's assistance with offers of accommodation for the various departments and within two weeks all the government offices were re-housed and open to the public. A Fire Fund was established and an account was opened at each of the banks to accept donations from the public. Many friendly nations also came to our aid with financial assistance, furniture and equipment. It took years to recover from this disaster.

With the encouragement and full support of the Minister for Communications and Works, Grenadians from all walks of life formed a 'maroon' one Sunday in December 1990 to assist in clearing the rubble from the burnt-out site. People donated their time, their trucks, food and drinks to assist in the massive cleaning-up project.

The government began the awesome task of rebuilding the complex. With the help of loyal citizens interested in preserving the aesthetic feature of the Carenage, plans were made, finance obtained, and rebuilding commenced in 1994. This was completed in record time, and the completed structure was officially handed over to the government of Grenada at an impressive ceremony which took place in September 1996. The Ministry of Finance and its related departments were re-established in a beautiful new structure, built in such a way that it blends in beautifully with the nearby Georgian buildings on the Carenage.

In August 1991 Grenada was returned as a member of the East Caribbean Supreme Court.

Mr Curtis Strachan CVO, retired as Clerk of Parliament on 30th September 1991 after 50 years of distinguished service in the public service of Grenada. He became the doyen of Commonwealth Clerks of Parliament. Although due to retire in 1986, he was asked to continue to facilitate Grenada's re-entry into the parliamentary democratic system after four and a half years of revolutionary rule. He returned to Parliament as Speaker of the House and in 1996 Sir Curtis was knighted by Her Majesty the Queen.

The name of the Grenada Public Library was changed in 1992 to the 'Sheila Buckmire Memorial Library' in honour of its longest serving librarian. Mrs Buckmire was well qualified and extremely efficient, creating many interesting and useful innovations to an archaic system. She died in 1985.

In 1994 Prime Minister Nicholas Brathwaite resigned as leader of the National Democratic Congress (NDC) and Mr George Brizan was elected as leader of the party.

The 1995 general election was won by the New National Party and Dr Keith Mitchell became our new Prime Minister.

Cuba's President, Dr Fidel Castro, visited the island state in August 1998.

Due to failing health, Mr George Brizan, the leader of the National Democratic Congress, stepped down and allowed the deputy political leader, Mrs Joan Purcell to lead the party at the January 1999 elections.

On this occasion the NNP received an outstanding victory at the polls, winning all 15 seats. Dr Mitchell became the first Prime Minister since independence to win two consecutive general elections. At his swearing-in ceremony he promised that safeguards would be put in place to ensure that his government was acting always in the interest of the country.

In November 1999 a severe sea surge brought by hurricane 'Lenny' in the northern Caribbean, caused much damage to the west coast of the island, eroding our beaches and destroying our sea defences and roads. Once again sympathetic nations have come to our assistance and a massive reconstruction project has begun on the main roads and sea defences on the west coast of Grenada. Many of our beaches have been rebuilt with sand from other areas and our tourists can continue to enjoy the beauty of this wonderful island.

Grenada has participated in several international fairs where the island's beautiful flowers and fruit are displayed. Ornamental bananas can be seen as well as anthuriums, ginger lilies, heliconias and other tropical blooms and ferns. At the commonwealth fair held in the UK in the year 2000, Grenada's booth was judged the most popular and colourful. Both flowers and fruit were on display as well as other products manufactured in Grenada – rum, nutmeg oil, etc.

For the last four years an exhibition has been mounted at the Chelsea Flower Show, also in the UK. The first year of the exhibition, a silver medal was won and for the last three years the award has been a silver-gilt medal for the beautiful and imaginative displays produced.

| 3 |
Our welcome to visitors

By air

Our international airport at Point Salines is within easy reach of all major hotels in the south of the island. Its 10,000 foot runaway can accommodate the largest commercial jets for both day and night landings.

American Eagle (a subsidiary of American Airlines) offers an ATR 72 aircraft carrying 64 passengers. They operate two flights daily Grenada/San Juan, Puerto Rico. The San Juan hub enables passengers to connect with most main US cities and points beyond, including South America.

LIAT (Leeward Islands Air Transport) offers 9 flights daily flying to most of the English-speaking islands of the Caribbean, as well as to Martinique and Guadeloupe. *British Airways* offers two weekly flights to and from London, England. *JMC* (formerly Caledonian Airways) offers charter flights twice a week from the UK to Grenada. *Air Jamaica* has two flights per day twice a week from Grenada to New York as well as to St Lucia and Montego Bay, Jamaica. *St Vincent & Grenada Airlines* (*SVG Air*) flies regularly between Grenada, Carriacou and Union Island and will accept charters to fly anywhere in the region. *Trans Island Air* flies from Barbados to Carriacou airport. *EC Express* flies every day to St Lucia, St Vincent and Barbados. *Caribbean Star* has daily connections with Antigua, Dominica, Port of Spain, Trinidad and St Vincent. *Rutaca* and *Avior* have a twice-weekly service from the island of Margarita. *Avior* also flies to other airports in Venezuela. *Condor Airlines* arrives from Munich, Germany once per week. A number of charters fly to and from Canada and Europe during the summer and winter months, e.g. *Royal Air, Sky Services* and *Canada 3000* operating from Canada once per week, and *JMC* from Britain.

Amerijet Intl. Inc., a cargo company, operates three days per week directly out of Miami and two days per week into Port of Spain, Trinidad. *Fine Air*, another cargo service, operates the Miami/Grenada route twice per week. The courier services of *FedEx, DHL* and *LIAT* all have regular flights into Grenada. Negotiations continue with other airlines as major expansions improve passenger and cargo handling in the future.

Even from the air, the beauty of the island is unsurpassed. The east coast faces the Atlantic Ocean where the waves, driven by the north-east trade winds, hammer the shore relentlessly, throwing up white spume as they crash into each other in their angry rush to the shore. The Caribbean Sea on the west coast is more placid, lapping gently at beautiful beaches formed in the many bays and inlets. The waters are exceptionally clear with hues ranging from the deepest azure to the palest green. Tiny houses can be seen clinging to the hillsides and nestling in the valleys amidst green carpets of lush vegetation. The runway is on a narrow peninsula and, as we land, the small off-shore islands conjure up pictures of deserted tropical islands with swaying palms and white sandy beaches where the sea, quietly lapping on the shore, would lull anyone into a pleasant state of mental and physical numbness.

By sea

The deepwater inner harbour in St George's is one of the most beautiful in the Caribbean. Ships enter through a channel between

Inter-island schooners, yachts and other craft are moored along the Carenage
(ROGER BRATHWAITE)

two promontories. On the left is Fort George dominating the entrance. On the hilltop to the right will be seen the burnt-out remains of Butler House, originally built as a hotel, but in the more recent past it was used by the People's Revolutionary Government as the Prime Minister's office. This building was burnt to a shell by members of the ruling party during the fighting in October 1983.

Ships normally dock at the pier, which can accommodate two large ocean-going vessels. The minimum draught here is thirty feet. Adjoining this is the Carenage (pronounced Ca-reh-nagh). In days of yore, before the road was built up, boats used to be careened here so that the undersides could be scraped and re-painted. The principal mercantile houses are situated around this bay and there is the continuous bustle of commerce during the week. The buildings appear to be constructed almost one on top of the other, up the slopes of the ridges that encircle the bay. Finally, there is the backdrop of hills, giving an air of protectiveness and tranquillity to the whole scene. On busy days, cruise ships are also berthed stern-on to the opposite side of the Carenage, but passengers normally alight by tender at the pier and begin their tours from that point.

Cruise ships are often welcomed by a steel band playing popular calypsos and, now and again, tunes more familiar to the visitor. The Grenada Board of Tourism has an office just outside the entrance to the pier. Our Cruise and Yachting Officer calls on all tourist ships to welcome visitors and to advise them on available tours.

Pleasure yachts sail into the lagoon in St George's or to Prickly Bay at the southern end of the island where they can clear immigration and customs, in and out, at no charge unless overtime is involved. This, of course, will have to be paid, including transportation costs for the officer concerned.

There are six yacht marinas in the State of Grenada. In the lagoon near to the town of St George's, a marina is operated by the Blue Lagoon Real Estate Corporation. They provide berthing for yachts and offer full services: water, electricity, shower and bathroom facilities, ice, etc. A twenty-four hour security service is in operation. Day chartering and term chartering can be arranged from this point.

At Prickly Bay, the Spice Island Marine Services Ltd has stern-to berthing for 25 yachts and provides full facilities. A 35-ton mobile hoist is available and the yard can accommodate about 25 yachts on the hard. There is also a sail loft, a ships' chandlery. Laundry and fax services are available, as well as diesel, electricity and water. The

Grenada government provides customs and immigration services at this point. There is a tiny shop on the premises with essential foodstuffs and other items, as well as a restaurant where satellite television entertainment is available.

The Moorings Ltd operates at Mt Hartman Bay and provides stern-to berthing for yachts up to 65 feet. There are 44 slips and two alongside for yachts about 17 feet with a draught of about 20 feet. Moorings are also available in the bay entrance channel which is marked but not lit. The dock has 110 and 220 volt power, 50 hertz. Water, petrol, diesel and propane are all available and there is a yacht caretaking service. Mechanical and electrical repairs are also undertaken. There is a customs office on site, as well as a mini-mart, and a convenient laundry service. The Rum Squall Bar has a happy hour from 5–6 p.m. daily. There is a dive shop close by, and for ships docked at the moorings, the use of the nearby hotel tennis court, beach club and swimming pool are available free of charge. Fax services are also available.

Further along the east coast at St David's Harbour, the Grenada Marine is a newly established marina, presently offering limited berthing with plans to increase their berthing facilities to 50 yachts by the end of the year 2000. Their boatyard offers a repair service together with fibreglassing and painting. There is a 70-ton 32-foot wide travel lift which is suitable for hauling even the many catamarans presently cruising in Caribbean waters.

The marina is being established on ten acres surrounding a naturally deep-water harbour with a barrier reef on either side. The low lying hills surrounding the bay keep it well protected from severe storms. There is a ships' chandlery; showers and laundry services are also available. The Internet café offers Internet access, Email facilities, etc. Diesel is available as well as electricity at 110 and 220 volts. There is also a mini-mart offering a small selection of groceries and other essentials. The Galley restaurant overlooks a small beach – an ideal place for having a swim before lunch or dinner.

True Blue Bay Resort has a small marina suitable for the docking of 20 yachts. No maintenance work can be carried out here, but fuel, ice and water are supplied. There are also twelve moorings in the

Grenada's police dressed in ceremonial regalia *opposite* (ROGER BRATHWAITE)

bay. Horizon Yacht Charters and Eco Dive both operate at this marina. The 25-room hotel nearby has a swimming pool, bar and small restaurant all of which are available to the crew on visiting yachts. The marina at Carriacou is also just being developed. There is already a haul-out facility for up to 50-ton monohulls, and a small storage area for repair work, cleaning and painting. A ships' chandlery will soon be opened and the fuel and water dock will overlook the mini-marina. It is planned that 14 yachts will be accommodated, and there is already a dinghy dock nearby. In close proximity to this development is an aluminium workshop and an engineering workshop, as well as a beach club providing accommodation with a bar, restaurant, an Internet café, tennis courts and showers.

Grenada coast guard

Grenada is the proud owner of a three-million-dollar 110-foot coast guard cutter called the 'Tyrrel Bay', as well as two Boston whalers, a 40-foot patrol boat and a rigid inflatable boat all used for general patrol duty around the islands. The coast guard performs a very valuable service, and there is on-going training for search and rescue operations, security, anti-smuggling, etc. Safety inspection on vessels is also undertaken when requested. The five marinas and the coast guard stand by on Channel 16 VHF. Any yachting amateur radio operators can be assisted in obtaining a reciprocal licence through the government wireless officer.

Immigration and customs

Our officers have been specially chosen and trained to welcome visitors and handle the necessary formalities as quickly as possible, and in a pleasant and efficient manner. For a visit of less than three months, citizens of Great Britain, Canada and the United States do not need to produce passports. A return air ticket and some form of identity with a photograph (driving licence, ID card) will suffice. All other nationalities need passports.

All personal belongings (clothing, etc.) are admitted free. Also, there is no restriction on the amount of foreign currency which can be brought into Grenada. A word of caution: some banking transactions require strict identification, preferably by production of more than one document, for example a passport, a major credit card or driving licence containing a photograph and/or specimen signature.

There are fixed charges for hiring taxis to and from the city and surroundings which have government approval. These rates are posted quite clearly in the arrival hall at the airport and can also be obtained from the Grenada Board of Tourism.

Driving licences

Any visitor with a valid driving licence must present this to the police traffic branch at the Carenage, near the fire station, and a temporary licence will be issued as required. This also applies to holders of international driving licences. Temporary licences can also be obtained at car rental offices.

In Grenada we drive on the left side of the road. The speed limit is 15 miles per hour in St George's and throughout the island's towns and villages. On open roads, the speed limit is 30 miles per hour. It is illegal to park or wait within thirty feet of a corner or junction.

Accommodation

Visitors can find any type of accommodation they require, from luxury hotel to inexpensive guest house. The prices can range anywhere from US$850.00 per day per person for a luxury suite, all inclusive, with private swimming pool, to US$30.00 per day per person for a small bedroom in a guest house, with probably very little view, but clean, tidy and comfortable. Most of the hotels are situated on or very near the magnificent beaches which abound on the south coast of the island. The guest houses are mainly in the city and its suburbs, but within easy reach of the beaches by bus or taxi. The meals there will be of the basic West Indian variety and quite tasty.

The Board of Tourism will be pleased to supply a list of available accommodation with up-to-date charges.

Public transport

Taxis are easily obtainable and, if your party is large, a minibus can be hired for a day's outing around the city or to other parts of the

island. The manager or a receptionist at your hotel can easily arrange this with little trouble, including a picnic lunch if this is required. The Board of Tourism can also help with any arrangements, including tours to the island dependency of Carriacou.

Buses and minibuses ply the Grand Anse route and some make daily trips to various districts in the country. They leave from the busy market square, or the nearby Esplanade, at all times of day. Don't expect them to be punctual. They leave when they are full, often stopping at any point on the road to discharge or pick up new passengers. Bus stops don't mean very much. Stopping is at the whim of the driver and at the request of the passenger and is always done with good grace and friendliness. This is part of the charm of the island.

It is a local custom to name each vehicle, and the choice of names can be quite entertaining. Those in vogue are:

HOME ALONE, ROAD RUNNER, GOD'S BLESSINGS, HOT ROD, HOT STEPPER, MEDITATION, ALL EYES ON ME, SHOCKING VIBES, NEW MILLENNIUM, NICE & EASY, OUT FOR JUSTICE, WELL YUH DUN KNOW, GREY BABE, GIRLS DEM SUGAR, 'D'GOLDEN RULES', GRANDSON

There is a saying used locally 'When God can't come, he does send'. It is amusing to see one of the mini-buses named 'GOD SENT'.

Foreign exchange

Our currency is the Eastern Caribbean dollar, which is fixed at an exchange rate of EC$2.70 to the US dollar. Selling and buying rates at banks will be a little higher and lower than this rate. Cash is exchanged at EC$2.67 to the US dollar. The four commercial banks are all members of the Eastern Caribbean Central Bank which determines the daily rates of all other foreign currencies for the seven island groups whose governments support the bank. These islands are: Antigua and Barbuda, Montserrat, St Kitts and Nevis, comprising the Leeward Islands, and Dominica, Grenada, St Lucia and St Vincent and the Grenadines, comprising the Windward Island group.

Cruise ship off the coast of St Georges *opposite* (GILLARD)

Banks and other financial institutions

Two international banks operate in the island, along with three indigenous banks, all of which can assist the visitor with the cashing of travellers' cheques, credit card operations, and exchanging foreign currency (notes – not coins) and any other transactions, foreign or local, that may be necessary. Barclays Bank PLC, a British bank, opened its doors here in 1837 as 'the Colonial Bank' and is the oldest financial institution in operation. Apart from the main office in St George's, there are sub-branches at Grand Anse, in the town of Grenville, and on the island of Carriacou. The Bank of Nova Scotia, a Canadian-registered bank, opened a branch in St George's in 1963. There is also a branch at Grand Anse.

Of the local banks, the Grenada Co-operative Bank Ltd is the oldest established, having commenced business in St George's in 1932 accepting minimum deposits of one penny (in those days our currency was tied to the pound sterling) as a way of encouraging thrift among the population with small incomes. It is still familiarly known as 'The Penny Bank'. Branches function in Grenville, Gouyave and Grand Anse.

The National Commercial Bank of Grenada Ltd was registered in October 1979. There are branches in St George's, Grenville, Gouyave, Sauteurs and Carriacou with a sub-agency in St David's. Their head Office is NCB House at Grand Anse.

The Grenada Bank of Commerce Ltd came into being in January 1983. Its main office is at Grand Anse, with branches in St George's and on the True Blue Campus of St George's University.

In the city of St George's all of the banks are located between Church Street and Halifax Street. The hours of business are generally

Monday to Thursday	8.00 a.m. to 3.00 p.m.
Fridays	8.00 a.m. to 5.00 p.m.

Four other local financial institutions operate here:

The Grenada Building and Loan Association in Church Street, whose main objective is the financing of housing for its shareholders.

The Grenada Development Bank Ltd, a government-owned institution on Melville Street through which funds are available mainly from the Caribbean Development Bank, to farming and other development projects. Their terms are more attractive than those offered by commercial banks for similar loans. There is also a branch in Grenville.

The National Development Foundation of Grenada is a non-profit-making organisation, formed with a USAID grant and local donations to assist small businesses with advice, guidance and/or finance in situations where there are insufficient assets to enable them to approach a bank. The foundation is doing very good work among the poorer members of the community who have ambition and ability but no money to purchase the necessary equipment and materials to put their businesses on a sound footing. The office is located on Lucas Street.

Capital Bank International Ltd is located on Grenville Street in St George's. Normal banking services are provided for deposits and withdrawals, but there are no facilities for encashing travellers' cheques.

There are also a number of off-shore banks operating on the island.

Clubs and service organisations

The Grenada Chamber of Industry and Commerce is very active and works hand in hand with the government in the interest of its

Country children still like to pose for the camera (MICHAEL BOURNE)

37

members and the community. Courses and seminars are conducted from time to time for the benefit of staff in the business sector. Panel discussions are also popular, to which the public is invited. The Chamber's offices are located at Mt Gay.

The Rotary Club of Grenada: luncheon meetings are held every Thursday at noon at the Flamboyant Hotel, Grand Anse.

The Rotary Club of Grenada-East, meets for lunch every Wednesday in the town of Grenville, St Andrews's.

Lions International is another service organisation. Meetings are held in their den at the Tanteen tennis court compound on the first and third Monday in each month.

Soroptimists International of Grenada: meetings are held on the first Monday in each month at the Anglican High School compound, Tanteen. Meetings begin at 4.30 p.m.

There is a senior citizens club which meets once per month at the YWCA building on Scott Street. Some form of activity is planned each month and picnics are very popular. This group also visits the old people's homes and children's homes, teaching crafts, taking the elderly on outings, etc. At Christmas time, gifts are brought to as many homes as it is possible and convenient to visit.

The Grenada Red Cross has an office at Upper Lucas Street in St George's.

The YWCA at the corner of Scott and Herbert Blaize Streets, is open every day and sometimes into the evening depending on whether meetings or other activities are taking place there.

The Grenada Jaycees, St John Ambulance Brigade and Grenada SPCA are also active organisations, as are the horticultural society and the orchid circle.

Youth clubs and associations

The Rotaracts – the junior arm of Rotary – meet twice per month. Their objects are to assist with small community projects.

The Scouts Association of Grenada has cub packs and troops of scouts and venture scouts, totalling about 45 units with approximately 1700 members in all. The Chief Scout is the Governor General.

The headquarters of the Girl Guide Association are situated at the Villa, on a hill overlooking the Carenage. The Governor General's wife is usually the president of the association.

We have 63 4-H Clubs in the island state with a membership of about 1800 boys and girls. These are connected with all other 4-H Clubs internationally and our group leaders have been participating since 1989 in the Rock Eagle Conference held annually in Georgia, USA. Their object is the citizenship training of agricultural youth, with projects like vegetable gardening, the rearing of livestock and poultry, sewing, handicraft, house-craft, cooking, baking and cake decoration. The clubs receive technical and material support from the 4-H Unit in the Ministry of Agriculture.

Private clubs

These are described more fully in Chapter 15. They are:

The Grenada Golf and Country Club
The Grenada Yacht Club
The Richmond Hill Tennis Club.

There are also several clubs for players of football, cricket, etc.

We have two craft lodges and one royal arch chapter. The Ancient Order of Foresters and the Odd Fellows are also represented on the island.

Churches

Several Christian denominations practise in Grenada including Roman Catholic, Anglican, Presbyterian, Methodist, Seventh Day Adventists, Jehovah's Witnesses, Pentecostal, Berean and Grenada Baptists, Church of Jesus Christ of The Latter Day Saints and the Church of Christ, Scientist. Times of services are normally posted on each church door.

Other religions represented are the Bah'ai faith in Upper Lucas Street, and the Islamic Centre at 712 Herbert Blaize Street in St George's.

| 4 |
Exploring the city and its surroundings

St George's, Grenada's capital city, is considered the most picturesque in the Caribbean. Coming from the south of the island or disembarking from a yacht or cruise ship, the entrance to the city is by way of the Carenage. The roadway sweeps in a semi-circle around the bay which is the most beautiful, natural harbour in the Caribbean. The houses rise step by step, clinging to the surrounding hills, the whole scene giving the impression of a vast amphitheatre.

Six forts were built on the ridges encircling the city. Only two remain to remind us of our strife-filled past.

The main commercial houses are based on the Carenage, as are a number of good restaurants. Some fine examples of Georgian architecture can be seen in several of these buildings. Water taxis are fun, and for a small sum you can be whisked across from one side of the bay to the other, or into the lagoon. This small harbour is usually crowded with pleasure yachts as it is known to be a safe anchorage in any storm. The Blue Lagoon Real Estate Corporation offers docking facilities and the opportunity to charter a yacht for a unique and pleasurable sailing experience around the island and in the Grenadines.

The Carenage is always a hub of activity with the mingling of the business community, civil servants, vendors, visitors and the public in general, as they hurriedly or leisurely go about the business of the day.

At the end nearest the pier is an office of the Board of Tourism with vendors' stalls nearby selling all manner of locally produced articles. On the opposite side of the road are two buildings housing the Port Authority and the Customs Department. The Grenada Postal Corporation is situated at the back of this complex. This is their main office and the Philatelic Bureau will be found here.

Returning to the Carenage after a visit to the Post Office we see on our right the fire station with its hose-drying tower at the back. Smaller buildings on either side house the Immigration Department and the Traffic Department where temporary licences are approved for visitors to drive on the island. Dotted along the Carenage are duty free shops selling perfume and cosmetics, jewellery and other interesting items.

Just about midway in the curve of the bay is the office of Cable & Wireless Grenada Ltd, a subsidiary of the worldwide communications group. The road branching off at this corner leads to Herbert Blaize Street, where we can see Marryshow House. This building was once the home of our great West Indian statesman, T. Albert Marryshow, often called the Father of Federation, which he always advocated for these small islands, envisaging the group as one nation. Fittingly, it is now the office of the Resident Tutor for the School of Continuing Studies of the University of the West Indies. There is a small, specialised reference library and, at the back of the building, a Folk Theatre which is used quite regularly for small, local performances.

Continuing along the Carenage there is a nice pedestrian walkway with comfortable benches made especially for the weary traveller who might like to sit awhile to admire the activity in the harbour. Here, a bronze statue lifts its arms heavenwards. This is a replica of 'Christ of the Deep', the underwater statue off San Fruttuoso in Italy. It was presented to the people of Grenada by the Costa shipping line in appreciation for the willing assistance given by the Grenadians when their ship, the *Bianca C* caught fire in our outer harbour and sank in 1961. Thanks to the number of craft ferrying passengers and crew ashore, no lives were lost. The spot where she sank is now a favourite place for scuba divers.

Continuing along the concrete walkway we find some restaurants where visitors can experiment with tasty local dishes like lambie (conch) or have a more familiar medium-rare steak! We can try a delicious rum punch or some icy cold local draught beer.

There is a very good supermarket and a small bookshop which is fully stocked with a fascinating range of books by all the well-known and lesser known authors. Souvenirs, films and postcards are also available here.

Several cannon have been sunk vertically into the ground on the sea side of the Carenage to serve as convenient bollards for the many vessels that use our harbour. There is a cannon firmly embedded into

The Carenage with its backdrop of houses built on the surrounding hills
following pages (ROGER BRATHWAITE)

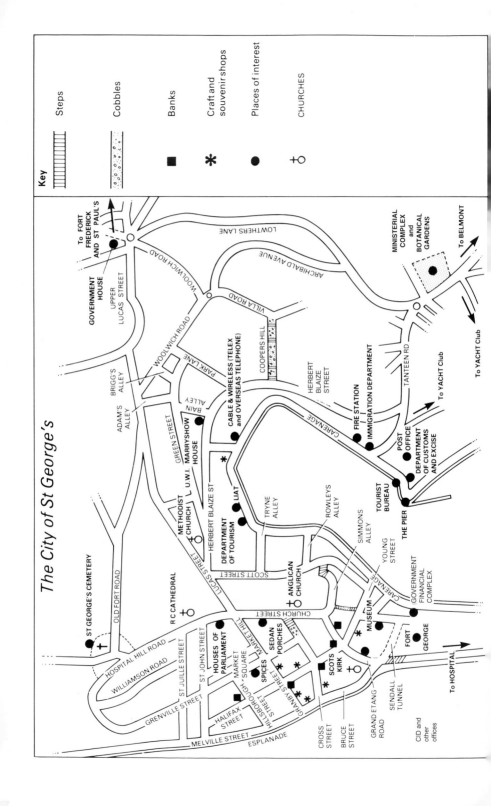

The City of St George's

Key

▨ Steps	
⋮ Cobbles	
■ Banks	
* Craft and souvenir shops	
● Places of interest	
○† CHURCHES	

The restored buildings of the Government Financial Complex
(ROGER BRATHWAITE)

the ground at the foot of Young Street as well. No one remembers when it was put there or why. Cannon will also be found at either end of the Long Wall in Lucas Street, and at White Gun, on the way to Richmond Hill.

The Public Library was established in 1846 and has been on its present site since 1892. There is a very good, up-to-date selection of books and magazines. The building is cool and breezy, with an excellent view of the Carenage, the pier and the lagoon.

Moving away from the Carenage, there are a number of craft and souvenir shops and other places of interest which will be mentioned here.

The Museum

The Grenada National Museum is housed on a portion of the ground floor of one of the oldest buildings in Grenada. It was erected in 1704 as a French military barracks. In 1763 the British converted it into the first prison on the island for both males and females. The

A peaceful anchorage for all sorts of craft can be found in the Carenage
(G. W. LENNOX)

tiny cells can still be seen. In 1880 the male prisoners were removed to Richmond Hill while the female prison remained in a part of this building until 1904. Early in this century, the first hotel on the island was constructed on this site, and the area now housing the museum was used at that time as a warehouse.

In the museum itself there are interesting artefacts from the era of the Siboneys, the Arawaks and the Caribs. You will see also some of our beautiful birds and butterflies. Old engines and the huge copper kettles used in the early days for boiling the cane juice are on display as are samples of the fabulous costumes worn at Carnival. These are only some of the many interesting exhibits here.

Sendall Tunnel
Completed in 1895 to join the two halves of the city, it is 340 feet long and about 12 feet high. Sir Walter J. Sendall was Governor of the

The statue of Christ of the Deep

island when it was commenced. He was a well-liked person and was responsible for many improvements around the island.

St Andrew's Kirk

A Presbyterian Church, popularly known as the Scots' Kirk, it was erected in 1831 with the assistance of the Freemasons. A small plaque was unveiled in their memory at the 150th anniversary of the Kirk in 1981.

Fort George

One of the many forts built by the French to protect their settlement on this coast, it was erected in 1706, the year after the town itself had been moved to its present site, and called 'Fort Royal'. When the British took over, it was renamed 'Fort George'. After the coup in 1979 the name was changed to 'Fort Rupert' (in memory of Mr Bishop's father who was shot during a civil disturbance in 1974) and on our return to democratic rule, we reverted to the name of 'Fort George'.

The Sendall Tunnel was built at the end of the nineteenth century to join the two halves of the city (SINCLAIR)

Visitors can climb up to the police headquarters which are based here. Further up is the Police Training School, and only on weekends are visitors allowed to see the old parade ground and battlements with their battery of cannon facing the outer harbour and the entrance to the inner harbour. The panorama is breathtaking.

At the end of this promontory is the General Hospital where once the military barracks were situated.

The Market Square

A lot of our history has taken place on this spot. It has always been a gathering place for the buying and selling of produce but, two hundred years ago, it was also used for public executions.

In the early part of this century, several respectable, middle-class families lived on the upper floors of the commercial buildings surrounding the square. It is a busy place every day of the week except Sunday. Vendors compete good-humouredly for your custom as attractive displays of vegetables and fruit catch the eye. For sale are yams, tannias, pumpkins and dasheen leaves to make those delicious callaloo dishes; green and dried coconuts; fruit-like golden

The hustle and bustle of the Market Square (ROGER BRATHWAITE)

apple, French cashew, sugar apple, passion fruit (which makes a lovely drink), and lots of citrus fruit all very temptingly arranged on wooden trays and tables. Bamboo brooms, cane baskets, hats, bags

A sample of locally made handicraft (ROGER BRATHWAITE)

and sun visors of straw, and all manner of spices and drinks can be purchased. In the background is the noise of buses coming and going, honking their horns, revving their engines, the drivers shouting to each other and to prospective passengers as they try to fill their mini-buses before departure. One thing is certain; they seldom leave on time!

The square was once a popular place for parades, political speeches and religious gatherings where excitable crowds were whipped into a frenzy of hatred or adoration.

The Minor Spices Society

At the back of the Market Square stands a building where all manner of aromatic spices can be purchased. Here will be found cinnamon, cloves, allspice, pimento and saffron. It is well worth a visit, if only to enjoy the pleasant aroma of the mixture of spices that pervades the atmosphere in this building.

Church Street

Three of the principal churches on the island are situated in this area. St Andrew's Kirk, which has already been described, is actually on Grand Etang Road adjoining Church Street, which stretches from the crossroads by Barclays Bank up to the cemetery, where the first hospital was built in 1738. This hill is still known as Hospital Hill.

Some very old buildings stand on Church Street, and there are still three excellent examples of sedan porches, used in the seventeenth and eighteenth centuries to shelter passengers from the elements when embarking or disembarking from sedan chairs. These were a popular mode of transport at that time. The porches then were open on either side to facilitate the entry of the chairs.

The Anglican Church

This was rebuilt in 1825 on the site of the original church constructed by the French Roman Catholics. The present clock, striking the Westminster chimes, was installed in 1904. Some very nice stained glass panels are seen here, as are some interesting memorial plaques. Three at the back of the church by the baptismal font were erected by the legislature of the day in memory of the Governor, civilians and soldiers who lost their lives during the Fédon Rebellion of 1795/96.

The Anglican Church on Church Street (MICHAEL BOURNE)

York House

This impressive old building has a very dignified past. Like many of our public buildings, it is not certain when this edifice was originally constructed and for what purpose, but as far back as can be remembered it has housed the legislature and the judiciary. It is believed to have been named after the Duke of York who visited Grenada in the eighteenth century. The Houses of Parliament are on the top floor, and visitors are welcome when Parliament is in session. The Mace of the House of Representatives is reported to be one of the largest in the world.

On the lower floor is our Supreme Court. Preliminary hearings and minor offences are dealt with in magistrates' courts which sit in each parish.

The Roman Catholic Cathedral

This was built in 1818 and has interesting stained glass windows and statues.

The Queen's Park

The park is one of the few large areas of flat land near to the city. It was donated to the people of Grenada by a Mrs Darbeau, and on 21st June 1887, the fiftieth anniversary of the accession of Her Majesty, Queen Victoria, it was officially handed over by the government of Grenada to the parochial board to be styled 'The Queen's Park' and converted into a place of recreation. The park has been used over the years for horse-racing, cricket, football, athletics, rallies and parades. A new stadium has recently been built. This will enable Grenada to host international matches at these grounds. In the cricket section there are three main stands and two bleachers that can hold in all about 15/20,000 persons. Inter-Caribbean and international matches are played here. When cultural events are to take place, a stage is constructed in front of the main stand. This serves well for rallies, parades and our carnival contests.

Another section of the field is used for football and athletics. Here, there are two main stands as well as the bleachers, capable of holding about 10,000 persons in all.

Richmond Hill

Leaving the city by the St Paul's route, we turn right at the White Gun. After a steep climb including rounding a hairpin bend, we finally arrive at the ridge on which the old forts were built. There were originally four, begun by the French after they recaptured the island in 1779 when it was realised that this site would command a larger area than either of the other two forts already in existence. They were completed by the British in 1783. The best preserved on this ridge is Fort Frederick. A climb to the old parade ground gives a spectacular view of the city and the outer harbour, stretching away to the southern peninsulas of Quarantine Station and Point Salines. On the ridge just below us is the prison compound, which was originally built as a military hospital. Higher still, up to the battlements, there is an even greater panorama over the hills and valleys surrounding this magnificent vantage point. The tunnels are closed now, but it is common belief that the forts encircling the city were at one time all joined by subterranean tunnels. Certainly sealed-off tunnels are to be seen at each fort and a little imagination can do the rest.

A colourful corner of the Bay Gardens *opposite* (G. W. LENNOX)

The Bay Gardens

These are yet further out of the city, but it is a pleasant drive. Here are excellent specimens of several tropical flowers, trees and fruit. The owners are very knowledgeable in the field of horticulture and are always willing to show visitors around for a small fee. You are quite welcome to wander around on your own. Specimens of our major crops grow there – nutmeg, cocoa and banana trees, together with spice trees like the bay, cinnamon and clove.

The Ministerial Complex
Botanical Gardens

This complex has been built in what was once the botanical gardens. These gardens were opened to the public in 1887 and by the turn of the century they were well established. Over the years some changes have taken place. Many interesting tropical trees and shrubs have had to give way to concrete structures and car parks. Apart from the Ministry of Finance which is on the Carenage, all the other ministries will be located on this site. At the entrance, there are still some remnants of what was once beautifully landscaped gardens. A war memorial now stands in this section, erected in memory of Grenada's sons who never returned from both world wars.

| 5 |

The west coast

Most official tours begin at the pier in St George's, but arrangements can be made to use any other venue. On this occasion we are going on a tour of the west coast. We cross the Queen's Park Bridge. This was originally known as the Green Bridge, named after Mr G. C. Green who was Administrator here at the time it was built. At that time it was also painted green. This structure spans the mouth of the St John's river, and was erected after a severe storm which completely demolished the previous bridge. After continuous showers, our rivers swell considerably and, to use a local expression, 'come down', bringing all sorts of debris including uprooted trees and animals. The raging waters sweep away everything in their path and have been known to carry small wooden houses, complete with occupants, far out to sea!

Our roads were laid out by the French when they were in possession of the island. They are all narrow and winding; it is said, jokingly, that goat tracks were used in mapping out the roads, as goats are known to choose the most easily accessible route up and down a hillside. As one soon comes to realise when driving in Grenada, we are either travelling up a hill or down a hill or at the foot of a hill.

Queen's Park itself is the venue for all important outdoor functions, as it is the biggest flat, open space near to the city. Large cultural events are held there, as well as cricket and football matches and athletics competitions. In the early part of the last century it was also used for horse-racing which was a popular sport at that time.

Leaving Queen's Park, we come to Cherry Hill. From here on the names bear testimony to our British and French origins. There are Fontenoy and Grand Mal, both on the same bay, which is ideal for a picnic and a swim. Then there's Monlinière, in which bay the French dropped anchor when they attacked and re-captured the island in 1779. Next is Happy Hill, then Beauséjour, an old estate, on through Brizan and encircling Halifax Harbour, a cove that is very popular with yachtsmen. It is sheltered enough to have been popular also

Halifax Harbour on the west coast of the island
(SINCLAIR)

with the pirates who roamed these waters in the seventeenth and eighteenth centuries. The anchorage is safe, and the swimming excellent. More often than not, yachts are seen anchored here, overnighting on their way further north, or sometimes just for a day's outing. The southern promontory overlooking the harbour is known as Morne Docteur. As we circle the cove, we pass along Perseverance estate, then to the northern end of the harbour we climb up to the boundary of another old estate known as Woodford.

It is a short drive from Woodford to Concord. The right fork in the road passing through the village would take us to the waterfalls on the Black Bay river known as the Concord Falls. There are three lovely waterfalls and reasonably sized pools for swimming. To get to two of them requires a bit of mountaineering, but the one nearest the road is a good place for a picnic. Each fall has a colloquial name. The first, spelt phonetically, is *Guea*. This is one of the patois words that it is difficult to translate. The nearest French word appears to be *guère*, meaning barely, or not much, but it would hardly apply to this fall in relation to the other two, which are of similar size. The second fall is around a bend in the river and is known as *Au Coin* – at the corner. The third, called *Fontainbleu*, appears to have a bluish hue in the mist that surrounds these falls.

A left turn from the main road leads to Black Bay. The sand here is quite black; a fine, volcanic sand, almost silky smooth compared with the larger grained yellowish/white coral sand of the other beaches. This is also a pleasant area for swimming.

Further on are small villages with names like Marigot, Grand Roy, Dothan and Palmiste. At Palmiste there's an open beach which is popular locally.

The sea, which can be so gentle, or so wild, is continually in motion, shaping, building up and destroying. Many portions of the road on this western coast were destroyed in the storm surge of 1999 and are being rebuilt. Our government spends a considerable amount on sea defences and maintenance. This is something that will always be a number one priority.

We are now in the parish of St John. Just before the town of Gouyave is Dougaldston estate where visitors are welcome. There can be seen samples of our main agricultural crops – cocoa, nutmeg and bananas. There might even be workers separating the nutmeg from the mace. Many spices will also be shown to visitors apart from the nutmeg. There is cinnamon, cloves and bay leaf to name a few. The old boucans will also be pointed out. These were used originally for the drying of cocoa beans.

It is interesting to note how the 'boucan' got its name. When pirates roamed the Caribbean Sea, they needed food that would last for the months that they remained at sea before coming into port to re-stock their vessels. Wild hogs roamed freely in the islands, particularly on the large island of Hispaniola, and these were hunted, killed and the flesh preserved by rubbing with salt, drying and smoking on a special frame in a type of hut known to the French as a 'boucan'. Wild cattle and fish were also preserved in this way. The pirates themselves became known as 'boucaniers' and the name was eventually anglicised to 'buccaneers'.

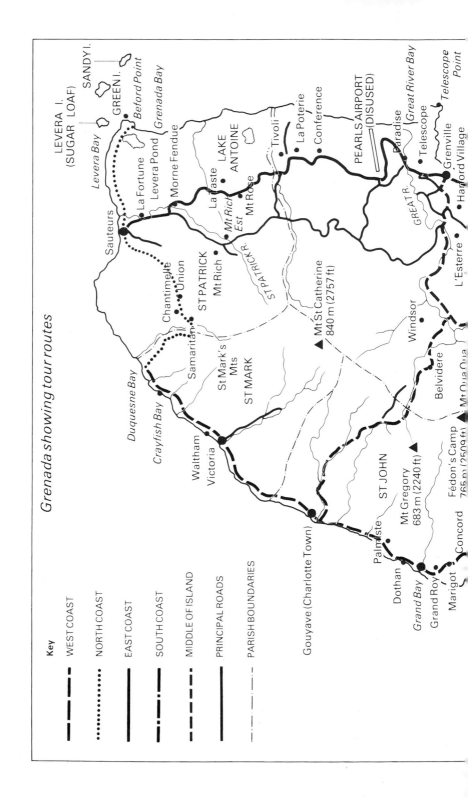

Grenada showing tour routes

Key
- WEST COAST
- NORTH COAST
- EAST COAST
- SOUTH COAST
- MIDDLE OF ISLAND
- PRINCIPAL ROADS
- PARISH BOUNDARIES

LEVERA I.
(SUGAR LOAF)
SANDY I.
GREEN I.
Beford Point
Grenada Bay
Levera Bay
Levera Pond
La Fortune
Morne Fendue
La Taste
LAKE ANTOINE
Mt Rich Est
Mt Rose
Tivoli
La Poterie
Conference
PEARLS AIRPORT
(DISUSED)
Paradise
Great River Bay
Telescope
Telescope Point
Grenville
Hanford Village
Sauteurs
Chantimelle
Union
Samaritan
ST PATRICK
Mt Rich
ST PATRICK R.
St Mark's Mts
ST MARK
Duquesne Bay
Crayfish Bay
Waltham
Victoria
Mt St Catherine
840 m (2757 ft)
Windsor
Belvidere
Mt Qua Qua
GREAT R.
L'Esterre
Gouyave (Charlotte Town)
ST JOHN
Mt Gregory
683 m (2240 ft)
Fédon's Camp
765 m (2509 ft)
Palmiste
Dothan
Grand Bay
Grand Roy
Marigot
Concord

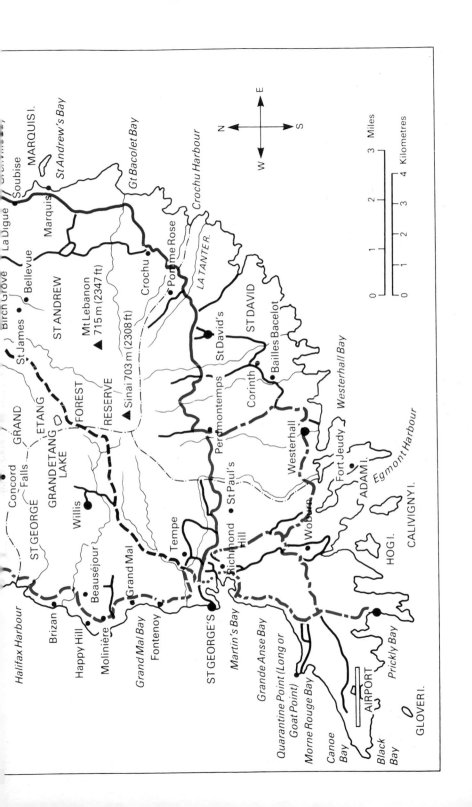

Cocoa drying at a boucan (SINCLAIR)

When the huge drying trays were built for cocoa, they were constructed on iron rails with wheels, so that they could be easily rolled into a roofed area during a shower of rain, and at night. The local farmers adopted the name 'boucan' for these 'drying houses'. Cocoa is now normally dried by machine, then sorted, bagged and shipped abroad for processing into cocoa powder and chocolate. Thus the boucans, once essential, are fast becoming a part of our past, giving way quietly to modern technology.

At Dougaldston estate also, visitors are shown nutmegs, mace and other spices like cinnamon, cloves and allspice. This is one of the estates that went heavily into the cultivation of bananas after the 1955 hurricane devastated its cocoa and nutmeg trees. Near the boucans, however, there are still some cocoa trees with their yellow and reddish-brown pods. When these are cut open we see the beans covered with a creamy-white substance which is quite tasty.

Concord falls on the Black Bay river *opposite* (MICHAEL BOURNE)

Gouyave

If anyone asks the direction to Charlotte Town, they would probably be met with a blank stare. The British tried their best to change the name of this small town when they regained control of the island from the French, and many of their earlier maps show the name as 'Charlotte Town'. Locally, however, it has never been accepted. Gouyave is the name of our town, and Gouyave it will remain. More recent maps show both names: 'Charlotte Town or Gouyave'. This town, the main one in St John's parish, has seen better days when owners of the nearby estates often owned a house in the town and transacted much business there, rather than having to take the long trip by horse and buggy into the capital. Those days have passed and the town is beginning to have a neglected air. The townspeople live mainly by fishing or employment on the nearby estates. The nutmeg processing station is the largest building. There, nutmegs and mace can be seen in their various stages of preparation prior to shipment. It is well worth seeing, and the visitor will enjoy the heady, pleasant smell of these lovely spices.

Up until the early 1930s, Belvidere estate in this parish was known to be the largest economically planned nutmeg estate in the world. In those days, the fields of nutmegs in Indonesia, in the Far East, our only rival, were not cultivated in any scientific manner. When the manager of Belvidere, a Mr Gurney, decided to switch from sugar-cane to the cultivation of nutmegs on a large scale, this was done with all the agricultural expertise available at the time. The result was the production of a high quality nutmeg which, with the other estates following suit, has made Grenada famous for the quality of this spice.

Belvidere was owned by the rebel leader, Julian Fédon, in the eighteenth century. It was at sea, off the town of Gouyave, that Governor Ninian Home and his party were captured during the Fédon Rebellion of 1795 and marched to the rebel camp at Belvidere.

Some tours turn off at this point and drive through either Windsor estate or Belvidere, and into St Andrew's. Driving through these estates, the visitor can see the fields of nutmeg and cocoa trees, banana plants and groves of citrus – oranges, grapefruit and mandarins. The drive on these unpaved roads can be a bit bumpy, but there is so much to see in this agricultural sector that the slight

The picturesque fishing town of Gouyave *opposite* (ROGER BRATHWAITE)

discomfort will hardly be noticed. On reaching St Andrew's, the tour returns to St George's by way of the Grand Etang road, passing the lake on the way back to the city.

Should you prefer to continue along the west coast, you will drive past several small settlements on the way to Victoria, the principal village in the parish of St Mark. This is the least populated district in the island, with about four thousand people.

Victoria is also a fishing community. It is an unforgettable experience to see the catch being pulled in at the end of a day. There is always a feeling of excitement and expectancy. The fishermen are shouting instructions to each other; crowds gather to enjoy the sport, shout encouragement to the fishermen and later on, to make their purchases; children are skipping happily up and down, getting in everybody's way and screaming excitedly. Like all small villages, the people of Victoria are friendly, and welcome a visit from strangers.

The lush valley at the foot of Mt St Catherine (GRENADA TOURIST BOARD)

Mt St Catherine, the highest peak on the island (2756 ft) is in this parish. A climb to the top can be arranged for the eager mountaineer. From the summit, all the parishes in Grenada are visible.

Sea birds frequent the fishing grounds off Gouyave and Victoria. Gulls, pelicans, terns and frigate birds glide aimlessly up and down in search of prey, diving for the catch and coming to rest on the rocks off the coast while their meal is digested.

Leaving Victoria, we pass through Waltham estate, along Crayfish Bay and on to Duquesne (pronounced du-cane). The beach here is a popular Sunday meeting spot for Grenadians living in the area.

From the parish of St George, we have travelled through St John and St Mark stopping at the border of St Patrick, the most northerly parish. In some of the small settlements that we pass, pigs and chickens can be seen walking around as freely as goats or sheep or children – all one happy family. The wooden houses often have no glass windows, but there would be shutters or what's known as a demerara window – a jalousied window pushed open and held by a long stick at the base of the frame These can be closed at night or during heavy showers. New concrete homes are in evidence, some built by Grenadians living abroad who intend to return. Some have already reached the age of retirement and have returned home to enjoy the twilight of their lives among their own folk.

A number of new homes have been constructed by local residents, often with assistance from relatives abroad. Many of these are built right next to the small wooden homes which no doubt belonged to their parents. The land is usually carefully divided between the children so that each can have a better start in life, owning a bit of the land that their parents worked so hard to acquire. We are all very family conscious, and with few exceptions, our old people are well looked after by their families.

| 6 |
The north coast

From Duquesne Bay, the road veers away from the coastline and continues inland through Union and Samaritan. Climbing the hill at Samaritan we can see, on the left, an old estate house – a typical house which was once occupied by the estate owners. Like most of these houses in Grenada, it is no longer maintained as an elegant home. Once, it was very well appointed, with beautiful gardens and lawns, tennis courts, riding stables and servants' quarters. The rooms were large and high-ceilinged for coolness. Very often there was beautiful moulding around the ceilings with exquisite lattice-work

Carib's Leap (ROGER BRATHWAITE)

Sauteurs Bay, a popular place for a swim and a picnic (MICHAEL BOURNE)

along the verandahs, on the window shades and around the stair-wells. Most homes had a front and a back verandah, all designed to keep the rooms cool. These homes were expensive to keep up and over the years the vast majority of them have fallen into disrepair – just proud ruins with little trace of their former glory.

We travel through Chantimelle and on to the town of Sauteurs on the north coast. This is the leading town in St Patrick, a parish with approximately 10,100 people. It is a small town, but well kept and tidy. Near the police station is the famous spot where the brave Carib warriors leapt to their death rather than surrender to the French in the mid-seventeenth century. Sauteurs Bay, to the west of the town, is an ideal spot for a picnic and/or a swim for any that prefer a more lively sea. From here can be seen the small islands which stretch between Grenada and the dependency of Carriacou. Isle De Ronde, immediately facing Sauteurs Bay, is the largest of these. In the towns and villages around Grenada, there are several small shops selling cold beers, soft drinks, and small cakes and biscuits. Continuing further west along this coast, the roads are unpaved, and have not

Sugar Loaf Island as viewed from Levera Beach (ROGER BRATHWAITE)

been very well maintained. There is a small private estate at Mt Rodney, and development land at Mt Alexander. Both these places provide magnificent views over the north and north-east coasts and, to anyone with an artistic eye, it would be well worth the miles of jolting along on a very rough track.

At Mt Rodney the old estate house has been renovated, and is now equipped to offer lunches to visitors. Local foods and fruit drinks form the basic part of the menu. Guests use a covered verandah from where can be seen the islands off the north coast of Grenada, stretching to Carriacou in the distance.

To the east of the town of Sauteurs and some distance from the town itself, another secondary road goes through to Levera Bay. Just before reaching the bay, there is a turn-off leading to another old family home which has been opened as a restaurant. It is called Helvellyn House. The grounds are nicely kept and the view is superb. On a clear day the island of Carriacou is visible in the distance. Local dishes are also included on the menu and these are attractively served and very pleasing to the palate.

The road to Levera is in just as poor condition as the one previously mentioned, but again as we near the coast the view before us is spectacular. From this vantage point we overlook three small islands

A deserted stretch at Bathway Beach (MICHAEL BOURNE)

which are very near to the mainland. The nearest is Levera Island, known to all locals as Sugar Loaf because of its shape. The second is Green Island and the one farthest away is Sandy Island. These are all privately owned, but a daytime visit can be arranged, usually sailing from one of the marinas on the south coast. The currents are strong here, and there can be much rolling at anchor. An overnight visit is not recommended, but as a lunchtime anchorage the trip can be quite enjoyable. Amateurs are advised against trying to snorkel in this area.

The road continues down to a very popular beach. There is always a strong breeze, and the waters are rougher than at any of the beaches on the leeward side of the island. Levera is tidal; only experienced swimmers please! Along the beach some perfect picnic areas can be found. This bay was used during the Fédon Rebellion in 1795 to discharge troops when it was found that the Grenville harbour had been blocked by the rebels and could not be used.

Just south of the bay is Levera Pond, which is the crater of an extinct volcano. Several species of tropical bird enjoy the undisturbed tranquillity of this forested area. Water hens, Caribbean coots, grebes and the belted kingfisher have all been seen here.

The ruins of the old fort at Bedford Point command another spectacular view. A small cottage industry in the Levera development area, making local style dolls of cloth and straw, is well worth a visit. Mrs Belingy has trained some young girls to assist her in what is becoming a thriving industry.

Lunch also can be reserved at an old estate house at Morne Fendue. Pepper Pot is a speciality of the house. This is a stew of several meats: beef, pork and chicken cooked with casareep, a preservative made from the cassava plant. In the days before refrigeration, this was how quantities of meat were preserved. The visitor will sample many other West Indian dishes, well prepared and attractively served.

| 7 |

The east coast

On this occasion we travel due east from the city, passing the Governor General's official residence, and on to White Gun, where good use has been made of an old cannon to mark the turn-off to the Richmond Hill area with its fort and prison. From this point also we can stop and look down into the Tempe valley where a number of factories are located, and on past to the Mt Gay hills in the distance.

The district of St Paul's, a suburb of St George's, is heavily populated. Here we should visit the Bay Gardens and enjoy a tropical extravaganza of flowers, fruit and spices in a beautifully landscaped setting.

A few nicely maintained private gardens in the area can also be seen by visitors for a small fee.

Along this route, some interesting places to visit would be the Camerhogne Art Gallery where local sculpture is on exhibit and for

Lake Antoine occupies the crater of an extinct volcano (ROGER BRATHWAITE)

sale and De la Grenade Industries where local fruits are made into jams, jellies and drinks. A delicious liqueur is also produced from local fruit. Another interesting visit would be to the Laura Herb and Spice Gardens which is cultivated by the Minor Spices Cooperative Marketing Society at Laura Lands in St David's. A small fee is charged and a guide takes the visitor around the gardens, pointing out the numerous herbs and spices that are grown in Grenada, and explaining their various uses.

The road twists and turns continuously along to Perdmontemps, then the curves become less frequent as we continue through Bailles Bacolet estate and on to Corinth and La Sagesse estates. Here, a secondary road leads to La Sagesse Bay, near which is the site of an old French village – Maigrin. The ruins are almost non-existent now.

At one corner of the bay a home has been turned into a small guest house and restaurant specialising in fish dishes. This was built by Lord Brownlow, equerry to the Duke of Windsor during his courtship of Mrs Simpson in the 1930s. The restaurant has a pleasant

A hat fashioned out of coconut fronds (GRENADA TOURIST BOARD)

ambience overlooking the bay. The meals are well prepared and nicely served.

A small nature centre has been developed there and hiking is encouraged along the cut trails. The beach is not overcrowded and is a pleasant place to relax and enjoy the sun and the sea air. The water however is very shallow and full of reefs in which shellfish abound. Nevertheless a sea bathe in the lively waters here is quite refreshing. Leaving La Sagesse, there is a gradual incline up to the police station at St David, a parish of approximately 10,200 people. The road levels off as we pass through Bellevue, Pomme Rose, Crochu and on to Grand Bacolet estate, then Hope estate. This last produces a large quantity of our coconuts.

The hills are less steep on this side of the island but the road is often some distance from the coast. However, several unpaved roads lead down to some attractive beaches and good picnic spots, perfect for those who enjoy exploring. From Hope, the road runs nearer the coast to the village of Marquis, where a type of large pandanus grass (or 'wild pine') grows in profusion at the seashore. The industrious villagers plait the dried grass into lengths which are eventually fashioned into hats, bags and mats. Marquis, or Le Marquis, was one of the first areas settled by the French, and it was here that the inhabitants were brutally massacred during the Fédon insurrection in 1795. Soubise is another little fishing community, and small boats are often seen being constructed here. The pace of life in these communities is much slower and calmer than that of the city dweller. Men and women have more time to meet with each other and to play dominoes and chat. The ground is bare, and often covered with nutmeg shells which provide excellent drainage. Animals wander around freely during the day but everyone in the village knows what belongs to whom. There's a sow with her litter enjoying a repast of banana skins; chickens scratching in the dust for a nice morsel of worm; a donkey tethered to a nearby tree, waiting for his master who has just stepped into the rum shop for a chat with his friends and an 'eights' – a local measure of strong rum, drunk in one gulp, not sipped, and followed immediately by a glass of iced water. This drink sears the throat, and inexperienced folk will probably end up coughing.

Modern technology appears even in the most remote areas. There's a TV aerial standing proudly on the roof of an unpainted wooden shack. It's a matter of getting one's priorities right.

The road continues along the coast to the town of Grenville, which is the principal town in the parish of St Andrew. On the northern end of Grenville Bay is Telescope. For many years a race course was maintained here, and meetings were held regularly at Telescope and at Queen's Park in St George's. The venue was eventually changed to Seamoon, the racecourse at Simon estate. To get there, we drive further north, over a bridge called Paradise, in a district of the same name, and take the right fork in the road. Paradise bridge was built in 1831. There are three lovely arches beneath the bridge, one large and two smaller ones. If we decide to walk down to the river using a path at the side of the bridge, no doubt there will be some women washing clothes there. It is easily accessible here, and has become a popular spot for clothes washing.

Horse-racing was held at Seamoon up until the late 1960s when it was found to be uneconomical to continue. Seamoon is now being developed into an industrial estate housing light manufacturing industries and local crafts.

Further on, we cross a Bailey bridge, built to take the place of an unsafe structure, and we arrive at the old airport at Pearls. This was closed when the new international airport opened in 1984. One can still visualise the activity that must have taken place here; the tearful

An archway under the nineteenth-century Paradise bridge (SINCLAIR)

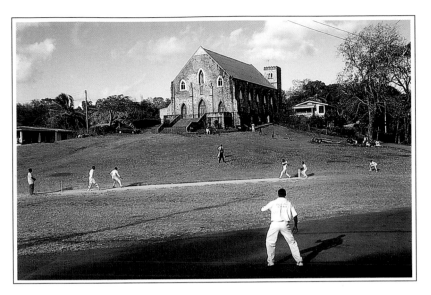

A fête cricket match in the grounds of the Tivoli Roman Catholic Church
(ROGER BRATHWAITE)

farewells, the excited welcomes, the constant flow of traffic, with vendors selling local fruit, nuts and sweets, and airport officials striding busily back and forth.

The buildings have been refashioned into site offices for various projects taking place in that part of the island. The busy scenes of the past have given way to more sober industry. There is no longer that hubbub of activity, but the place is still alive.

The road runs parallel to the runway then continues north. Amerindian artefacts have been found in the Pearls area but no excavation is allowed without government approval. The International Association for Caribbean Archaeology claims that the Pearls site is not only unique in the density of its archaeological content, but it is also the largest prehistoric settlement in the Lesser Antilles. It is believed to have been settled in the fifth century BC and was inhabited continuously by thousands of Amerindians until 12 AD. The Association estimates that the area settled was about 30 acres to the north of the old airport. There is a beach here also, good for a picnic, but the sea is very rough and not suitable for swimming.

Crossing to the west of the airfield, we continue north through Conference to Tivoli. A secondary road to the east leads to the village of La Poterie where, in keeping with its name, a suitable clay has been found for the moulding of pots, but there is no evidence that this has ever been used.

We can continue on to River Antoine estate, with its well-known rum distillery. Lake Antoine, in this area, is another lake which has been formed in the crater of an extinct volcano, and is a good place for bird watching.

Back on the main road, we cross over into the parish of St Patrick, driving through Pointzfield estate, Mt Rose, La Taste and Plains estate. There are small sulphur springs at several areas on the north coast but to get there usually necessitates a trek through a forested area and on occasion this can be quite slippery underfoot. The pools of warm water are not very large, and there are small fissures all around, emitting sparse clouds of sulphur-smelling vapour, but not enough to make it overpowering. Consideration is being given to incorporating one of these into a health spa scheme.

To the west of Plains is Mt Rich estate, where Amerindian artefacts have also been found, including a huge rock with primitive carvings. This used to be a great attraction, but the rock has slipped and is no longer as easily accessible.

We continue along the Plains road past Morne Fendue, La Fortune and on into the town of Sauteurs on the north coast.

There are several good picnic areas at the beaches on this east coast, but the sea can be quite rough.

| 8 |
The south coast

Leaving the city by the Lagoon road, we can see any number of pleasure yachts at anchor in the lagoon. Private yachts carry almost every flag in the world and come from as far away as Australia and New Zealand. The charter yachts normally sail between the Leeward and Windward Islands, going as far north as Antigua and as far south as Grenada. Our lagoon is well protected and a haven for yachts during a storm. The marina there provides facilities for visiting yachts. The commercial sector has spread to this area. There is a nice spacious supermarket conveniently situated opposite the marina and a small jetty nearby allows yachtsmen and women easy access. A bit

A peaceful early morning scene at Grand Anse Beach (MICHAEL BOURNE)

further along, just past the traffic lights going south, a visit can be made to Arawak Islands Ltd. This is a small manufacturing industry producing perfumes, soaps, body oils, condiments and insect repellants all from local ingredients. Local grasses and barks are packaged as well for the making of teas. There are some very attractive gift items and many of the local teas are pleasant and worth tasting.

Following the coast for most of the way, we arrive at Grand Anse beach. A conducted tour would take you to the southern end of the bay, but there are many access roads to this two-mile-long stretch of beach, and swimming in the crystal clear waters can be enjoyed safely at any point in the bay. The beach is of fine white coral sand, dazzling white in the midday sun. From the shore it shelves a bit then drops steeply away like a giant swimming pool. The water is so clear that you can see far down to the sandy bottom. The beauty of it all is that our beach is not crowded. No need to step over bodies while you try to find a spot to relax and enjoy the sun. This is naturally a popular spot for hotels and rental cottages.

The promontory at the southern end of the bay is called Long or Goat Point, but is popularly known as Quarantine Station. The buildings here were constructed as a hospital for the soldiers who had contracted that fatal disease of the nineteenth century, smallpox. These houses were maintained by the government and eventually turned into a holiday resort for Grenadians to enjoy an inexpensive holiday. They have now fallen into disrepair, and a radio mast has been erected on the site to strengthen the signal from the local radio station.

On the hill above the promontory a number of holiday cottages have been built for rental, and they have a fabulous view overlooking Grand Anse to St George's with the mountains in the background. From here, a very poor secondary road curves around Morne Rouge Bay to the place which, in the nineteenth century, was used as a leper settlement. This has not been in operation for at least a hundred years, and only the foundations of the building remain. There is also a beautiful view from this point.

With a sturdy vehicle it is possible to joggle along to Point Salines, but we would suggest the less hazardous route by the well-paved road leading to the airport. Just before the airport is the entrance to one of our major hotels. At the back of the airport and up the hill, the control tower is located. Further along the road is an all-inclusive

A deserted beach along the southern coast (MICHAEL BOURNE)

resort, beautifully landscaped with a tennis court, mini-golf course and swimming pool apart from a lovely stretch of white sandy beach. The bays at this southern end are not as sheltered as Grand Anse and the sea tends to be more lively but still enjoyable. Apart from the small restaurant at the airport itself, there are two very nice restaurants in the area worth seeking out.

At this end of the island there are also a number of residential developments on the many peninsulas that abound on the southern coastline.

True Blue, the promontory nearest to Point Salines, was the site used for the 'Carifta Expo' 69', the first international exhibition to be held in the Caribbean. The remains of the roadways and foundations of buildings erected at that time are still to be seen, but new homes are gradually appearing.

The main campus of St George's University is also on this point. This university has been in existence for nearly 25 years. It began as a medical school branching out eventually to include schools of arts and sciences, veterinary medicine and graduate programmes. There are about 1500 students registered at any one time for the various courses offered.

In the school of medicine the fifth and sixth term students relocate to St Vincent and their clinical training is conducted abroad. Apart from the resident lecturers, assistant and associate lecturers and instructors, there are a number of visiting professors from time to time who add their knowledge and expertise to an already well-rounded programme.

This university is recognised by many prominent institutions in the USA, the UK and other Caribbean islands.

The most populous site is Lance Aux Epines. Until the 1950s this was a farm, raising sheep and cattle, and there was only the owner's house which overlooked Prickly Bay. As people began to move out of St George's, and emigrants were searching for sites on which to build, this land gradually became too valuable to farm, and bit by bit it was cut up and sold as building lots. Four hotels have been built in this area, and there are several apartments and cottages catering to the holidaymaker. The beaches around are not our best, but they are still put to good use. The homes here are owned, by and large, by local businessmen and professionals, and retired people from North America and Europe.

Calvigny Island as viewed from Woburn (ROGER BRATHWAITE)

Coming back from Lance Aux Epines, we turn right and drive through woodlands where there is a small factory grinding sugarcane for the manufacture of rum. The Grenada Sugar Factory Ltd produces rums of different strengths to suit every palate. Old Grog is aged for 8 years and is 43% proof – a very popular rum. Their Special Dark and Superior Light have been gold medal winners at the rum tasting competition held in Barbados annually. A spice liqueur is also manufactured as well as a rum punch, spicy rum and rum lemon. Their hospitality centre is open Monday to Friday from 8.00 a.m. to 4.00 p.m. and sometimes on Saturday and Sunday depending on tourist demand.

Another right turn takes us through the fishing village of Woburn. There's a nice view of Hog and Calivigny islands before we turn inland to join the eastern main road. From this, we can branch off again to the right, to visit Calivigny Point where the main camp of the People's Revolutionary Army was located during the rule of Maurice Bishop's People's Revolutionary Government. This was heavily bombed during the intervention in October 1983. From this vantage point we again look out at the islands of Hog, Calivigny and Adam, all privately owned. A day's sailing trip to any one of these can be an unforgettable experience. There is always a strong, steady breeze that makes for enjoyable sailing, and very good anchorages at Hog Island, Calivigny Island, Prickly Bay, Egmont Harbour and Chemin Bay. As a matter of fact, this coast is full of harbours which provide safe anchorages, and with the normally dry climate on the south coast, it is ideal for holidaymakers and yachtsmen and women. There are plenty of reefs which afford excellent snorkelling to the enthusiast. Glover Island is another interesting spot where stand the ruins of a Norwegian whaling station.

Continuing our drive, the next point is Fort Jeudy, the site of an ancient fort which protected the entrance to Egmont Harbour but which is now in ruins. The harbour itself is a hurricane haven for yachts. During the reign of the People's Revolutionary Government the harbour was cordoned off and no yachts were allowed in, but this is all in the past.

Fort Jeudy is a residential development area and a few attractive homes have been built. The promontory is windswept, with trees and shrubs showing the effects of the constant battering that they receive. Waves crashing against the rocks and the shore, flinging spray high into the air, create a picturesque scene.

Still further along, we cross into the parish of St David and visit Westerhall Point, another area of residential development where more expensive homes were built by retirees from abroad who could afford to spend four to six months each year in their 'island in the sun'. Over the years, for various reasons, political and otherwise, many of these homes have changed into the hands of Grenadians. This peninsula is tastefully landscaped and the private road and grounds are well maintained. We can continue along this road and return to the city through St Paul's or back-track a part of the way then drive up to the Richmond Hill ridge overlooking the city. Another alternative would be to take what is known as the Springs road which overlooks the valley where the old sugar factory proudly dominates the nearby buildings. This is an area of small homes and miniscule gardens. Now and then there is a church, a playing field, a school. Too soon we rejoin the road that takes us back into the city.

| 9 |
Through the middle of the island

We can leave St George's either from the Esplanade and through River road, or by driving to the roundabout on the far side of Government House and down through the Tempe valley to River road. This valley area was the scene of much fighting during the 1983 disturbances, as an army camp was stationed in the surrounding hills. However, all is quiet now, and this is the main road which will take us, as we say 'over the Grand Etang' and to the other side of the island. In fact, we will be driving more or less through the middle of the island, from coast to coast.

Grenadians, when not at work, spend a lot of time out of doors, and we may come across a group of young men playing dominoes, or a 'wayside barber' giving a friend a haircut under the shade of a

Heliconia (ROGER BRATHWAITE)

tree, while pleasant conversation continues with their friends who relax comfortably nearby. There may be evidence of women's industry with brightly coloured garments neatly laid out to dry on hedges or hung on lines stretched between two trees, after being thoroughly scrubbed clean in a nearby river. Even the stones in the rivers are used for bleaching and drying.

The route to Annandale falls branches off from this road. Near the falls there is a rest house with changing rooms and washroom facilities which can be rented for a day's outing. The water in the pool at the base of the falls is cool and bracing, and much enjoyed by locals and visitors alike.

Back on the main road we pass through several villages where youngsters can be seen playing football or cricket, depending on the time of the year and the popularity of the game. Most of the houses are tidily kept with small neat flower gardens.

On the slopes of the Grand Etang range of hills, teak and fir trees are planted. There is also a profusion of rock fern which is very popular in all sorts of decorations and flower arrangements. The trees were planted after hurricane 'Janet' in 1955, when the island was stripped almost bare of its forests, and hundreds of acres had to be replanted. A denuded trunk here and there still bears testimony to this devastation, but in our fertile soil regrowth was rapid, and most of the dead trees were quickly hidden by vines, ivies and other plants. In between all the lush vegetation can be seen the bright red sheaths of heliconia plants which grow wild in this area. The road is narrow, and snakes its way up the mountainside. We look down into the valleys and up at the numerous peaks which change position as we drive along, like dancers in a chorus line. At certain times of the year the continuous droning of cicadas can be heard. These are large, broad insects of the *Homoptera* family, locally known as 'Coq Soleil'. They are heard with increased volume at the end of the dry season. The males produce this high pitched drone by vibration of their abdominal organs.

Much action took place in these hills during the fighting in October 1983. After the route became safe for civilian traffic, no less than seven vehicles were seen, all bullet-ridden and completely beyond repair; some had obviously been abandoned in a hurry, others had smashed into the hillside while trying to turn one of the sharp, steep corners. It is quite an unnerving experience to see the aftermath of a battle.

St Margaret's waterfalls (ROGER BRATHWAITE)

At the highest point on the road – 1910 feet above sea level – we can stop to look back and enjoy the breathtaking panorama of the forested hills and valleys, stretching far away to the southern tip of the island. The farther peninsula is Point Salines, where the new international airport is located. The nearer point is Long or Goat Point, commonly known as Quarantine Station, curving into Grand Anse Bay. You will want to spend some time here just drinking in the beauty all around; the myriad shades of green, interspersed with flaming reds and yellows of the poui trees; tiny houses dotted here and there in the vastness of the green landscape. Slivers of white are

The deep waters of the Grand Etang lake lie in the crater of an extinct volcano (G. W. LENNOX)

just discernible on a clear day, showing the small beaches that are scattered around the southern peninsulas.

Grand Etang Lake is the crater of an extinct volcano. To this day, some people will claim that it is bottomless, but this has been disproved by various experts who have conducted surveys over the years.

Just above the lake is the headquarters of the Forestry Department. Until recently, a small police station operated here but this was closed during the era of the People's Revolutionary Government. The larger building houses the Forestry Interpretation Centre. Here we can stop for some refreshment and enjoy a cooler temperature while inspecting samples of our agricultural produce, forestry and handicrafts. This building was originally a holiday home rented out by the government. It was turned into an army barracks by the PRG and the building was a complete ruin by the end of 1983. The restoration of this area has been made possible with assistance from the US Agency for International Development.

The Grand Etang is a government forest reserve. Wild game abounds in the forests, and consequently this is a popular camping area for hunters. From the lake there is a slow descent to the village of Birch Grove. On the higher slopes, nutmeg trees are very much in evidence and, as we descend, these give way to cocoa trees and banana plants. We see groves of bamboo too, with their creaking stems and long, delicate-looking leaves.

A number of nature trials start from this point – in a northerly direction to Mount Qua Qua from where there is a commanding view of many parishes: to Fédon's camp where the rebels executed their prisoners during the 1795/96 rebellion; across the hills to the west coast and Concord falls; or in a southerly direction to St Margaret's falls. Some of these are narrow and precipitous and the inexperienced or faint-hearted are advised to think twice before attempting any of them. However, there are many shorter, safer trails that can be enjoyed by all. Experienced guides are available at the Grand Etang Interpretation Centre, or arrangements can be made through the hotels with one of the tour operators.

About half way down, an unpaved estate road branches off to the right. This is one of the starting-off points for a visit to St Margaret's falls. That journey should be undertaken only by the young and adventurous. The path becomes extremely narrow, slippery and precipitous and necessitates travelling in single file for most of the way. The falls are pretty, but not as high as the Annandale falls.

Downhill from the Grand Etang road, and across the valley, there is an excellent view of Mount Qua Qua. This range of hills, farther to the north, featured greatly in the fighting during the Fédon Rebellion of 1795/96.

It would come as no surprise to see a goat or sheep lying in the middle of the road. A toot of the car horn, and the animal will get slowly to its feet and amble away quite unconcernedly. They are accustomed to vehicular traffic, and at any time might decide that the grass is greener on the other side of the road. They have not learnt to look at the left and right before crossing.

At the village of Birch Grove there is a small police station near the bridge. The river that we cross here is well-known for its abundance of crayfish. This is like a giant freshwater shrimp, related to the lobster family, and considered quite a delicacy.

Across the bridge, we can turn right and drive over the hills through St James, La Digue and Harford Village, which is picturesque.

The jetty at Grenville (SINCLAIR)

We might prefer, however, to continue straight along until, at a corner, we arrive at a small shop called the 'Traveller's Rest'. There is not much room for actually resting, but we can purchase a cold bottle of beer or a soft drink before recommencing our journey.

We drive through Balthazar estate, crossing over a river which bears the same name. Our rivers are not very large and some people would consider them mere streams, but that's all that we have and, to us, they're rivers! The L'Esterre causeway is an interesting piece of construction. It was specially built so that the river could run over and under without damaging the structure. Seeing the waters in the river running between the rocks so far down, no one would believe that, after very heavy showers, this same river can swell to cover the causeway by as much as half a metre. At these times, rocks and uprooted trees and all sorts of debris come rushing down in the raging torrents, and the causeway has to be solid enough to withstand this onslaught. On one such occasion, we had to wait for over two hours before the waters subsided enough to enable us to drive across.

The cocoa receiving station at Carlton can be a worthwhile stop. Here, the cocoa beans are purchased, dried and sorted ready for shipment. A lovely chocolatey aroma pervades the whole building.

On the approach to the town of Grenville, the white foam from the breakers can be seen as the waves hit against the coral reefs which make the harbour so dangerous for shipping. The seasoned captains know the entrance between the reefs, but it would be foolhardy for newcomers to attempt to find their way through. Many a vessel has come to grief on these sands. This area was originally known as La Baye and is still known locally by that name.

Grenville is a quiet town. It is the principal town in St Andrew, an agricultural parish of about 22,500 people. Most of the activity takes place on Victoria Street, the main street which faces the waterfront. The banks which serve this community are housed in the most imposing buildings on the street. On the waterfront, small stands have been erected where the day's catch of fish is sold as the fishermen come in. The police station is near by, no doubt to discourage any misunderstandings that might arise over the price of fish!

The Grenville market, behind the Court House on Albert Street, comes to life on a Saturday when the agricultural farmers bring their vegetables and fruit to sell, and the livestock farmers bring their

The court house at Grenville (SINCLAIR)

chickens and pigs. There are butchers right on the spot selling beef, veal and pork, all of which have been freshly slaughtered. The mood is lively as friends meet and exchange bits of gossip and discuss their purchases. The vendors also enjoy themselves, encouraging the hesitant shopper and forever re-arranging their produce to make as attractive a display as possible. Dogs roam around looking for the odd titbit. They frequent the butchers' stalls because the scraps that are thrown away there are the most tasty! Young boys walk around offering land crabs all tied together with strong grasses. These are sold alive and are very popular as an addition to our callalou soup.

There is a nutmeg receiving station and a processing plant where the mace is dried and the nutmegs are sorted and made ready for shipment. The workers are quite willing to show visitors through the plant.

The Anglican church is a pretty little building set in its own small grounds on Victoria Street. It takes little imagination to realise that these streets were named during the reign of Queen Victoria.

There are a number of small but reasonably good places in the town where a meal can be purchased – a hamburger, salt fish and bakes (if you care to go local), or a simple meal of chicken or beef with possibly rice and a salad. None of these places is open on a Sunday, but a picnic lunch can easily be supplied by your hotel before leaving St George's.

| 10 |
A trip to Carriacou

Carriacou is the largest island in the Grenadine chain which stretches between Grenada and St Vincent. The island boasts a population of approximately 4700 on an area of about thirteen square miles. There is a central ridge from which the land slopes down to the windward and leeward coasts.

Responsibility for this island chain is shared between Grenada and St Vincent. In determining administration, an imaginary line was drawn and it was agreed that all the islands north of this line would be under the control of the St Vincent government, and those to the south would fall under the jurisdiction of the government of Grenada. Thus, Carriacou and Petite Martinique form part of this island state. The imaginary line, which not too accurately follows a line of latitude, slices off the northern tip of Carriacou and also of Petite Martinique, so if you walk to Rapid Point, or Gun Point as it is known locally (because of the cannon in place there), you would actually be in St Vincent territory!

Like Grenada, agriculture and fishing are important to the economy of the island, but the days when large quantities of cotton and sugar-cane were produced are a thing of the past. There was a time when Carriacou produced the best bred ponies in the Windward Islands.

Some vegetables are grown for local consumption and supplemented with the importation of other fruit and vegetables from St Vincent and Grenada. Groundnuts (peanuts) are cultivated in quantity and supply the Grenada market. There is a lively export trade in fish and sheep to Trinidad.

Tours to Carriacou can easily be arranged through one of the travel agencies in Grenada, or by chartering a yacht from one of the marinas. Visitors might prefer to 'go their own way' and choose to fly or take a trip on a local schooner.

The airfield at Lauriston is small, and aircraft fly in daily, some days having two scheduled flights. The flying time from Point Salines to Lauriston is about twenty minutes. Schooners ply regularly from the schooner wharf in St George's harbour to Hillsborough, the main town in Carriacou. They sail on Saturdays and Wednesdays, returning to Grenada on Mondays and Thursdays (holidays excepted). These inter-island schooners range from about 30 to 60 feet in length, and

Hillsborough Harbour on the island of Carriacou (GRENADA TOURIST BOARD)

carry an amazingly wide assortment of passengers and cargo. We can see uniformed government officers and well-dressed businessmen and women, vendors, workmen and tourists, in close proximity to live chickens, sheep, baskets and sacks of vegetables and fruit, all bound for the same port. This is a good way for visitors to get to know the friendly islanders. The journey takes about four hours, and the sea can be as calm as a pond, or very rough, depending on the time of the year and, of course, the weather.

There are two large catamarans now plying the St George's/Carriacou route in a much shorter time. The *Osprey Shuttle* journeys between Grenada and Carriacou daily, taking $1\frac{1}{4}$ hours. This vessel can hold 250 passengers. The *Lexiana Jet Express* also plies this route on a regular basis, and can accommodate 260 passengers for the $1\frac{1}{4}$ hour crossing.

The most relaxing of all journeys would be by yacht, cruising comfortably from one of the marinas in Grenada. Sometimes the yachts overnight in Halifax harbour, then sail on to Carriacou the following day. This journey under sail can take the better part of the day in good weather, and it is an exhilarating experience. Travelling up along the leeward coast can be very pleasant and relaxing, passing all the coastal towns and villages that may have been visited previously by land when touring the west coast.

As we clear the northern tip of Grenada the north-east trade winds welcome us in full force. We skim past Ile de Caille with its whaling stations in ruins; Ile de Rhonde, the only inhabited island in this group; Les Tantes; and we are nearing Diamond Islet, known locally as 'Kick 'em Jenny'. Our sailors say the rock got this name because the waters around it can kick like a mule, but it is probably a corruption of the French *Quai que gêne*. Currents travelling east meet west-bound currents near this rock and the waters here can be the roughest in the entire Grenadine chain. On the other hand, I have sailed past when it has been absolutely still.

There are sea birds in plenty whose nesting places are among the many rocks and smaller islands, covered with guano, which lie between Grenada and Carriacou.

As we near our sister isle, we pass the islets of Mabouya (meaning evil spirit in the Carib tongue) and Sandy, which is slowly being eroded by the sea, and enter Hillsborough harbour. This bay is large, crescent-shaped and very exposed. Yachts seldom overnight there as the continuous swells make for an uncomfortable night.

The town of Hillsborough is built in the curve of the bay, with Main Street running parallel to the shore. Here, at the head of the pier, are the customs and immigration, government offices, the post office, police department and the market. Sunday after church is a favourite time for visiting the market to make purchases and pass the time of day with friends. Mondays and Thursdays are also busy market days.

There are two banks, both on Main Street, and several small shops. The accommodation in Hillsborough is comfortable and tasty local meals are served. Fish and lobster are plentiful in the Grenadines and the islanders make an excellent job of cooking them. A tiny museum exhibits artefacts unearthed from various parts of the island.

A guided tour can easily be arranged to many places of interest in Carriacou. The villages have either French, English or Scottish names as proof of the first European settlers to own property here.

This small island has over eighty miles of roadway, all originally built by the French, as were the military fortifications which have now disappeared. One fort overlooking Hillsborough has been turned into a waterworks, and the cannon are relocated on Hospital Hill as an attraction to that site. When the French were in possession of the island, there was often no naval support, hence the reason for the vast network of roads which enabled them to transport their artillery speedily from one place to another in their continual fight against the British invaders.

On a hill a few miles north of Hillsborough is the hospital. The view from here is absolutely breathtaking. With cannon pointing out to sea, we look down on the town of Hillsborough nestling close to the wide sweeping arc of the bay, and way beyond to the airport at Lauriston, the tiny islands south and on to Grenada in the distance.

Travelling south out of town, we arrive at Harvey Vale, near which we can see the tree-oysters in the mangrove swamp by the shore. These molluscs attach themselves to the roots of the mangrove and live happily in the briny water. The bay in this area is known as Tyrrel Bay. It is far more sheltered than Hillsborough and considered an excellent anchorage. A small marina is being built in this area. In and around the village of Harvey Vale small cottage and apartment hotels have sprung up, as well as some nice restaurants. All manner of water sports is available including scuba diving and snorkelling. The numerous reefs around these islands afford the diver spectacular underwater scenes.

Work boat race in the annual Carriacou Regatta (ROGER BRATHWAITE)

From here we can turn inland and drive to Six Roads, a junction from which roads branch off to different parts of the island. Carrying on to Top Hill, there is an exceptionally good view of both sides of the island, then down and through Mt Pleasant and Limlair, we finally arrive at Windward, an apt name for this area with the trade winds a strong and constant presence.

At Windward, the descendants of Glaswegian shipwrights still practise their trade and most of the fishing boats and inter-island schooners are built here. White cedar is used for the vessels, while dogwood (a tree peculiar to Carriacou and not found in Grenada), is used to build the keel. Names like McDonald, McFarlane and McLawrence are still very much in evidence, and they are all proud of their Scottish ancestry.

The road from Gun Point along the western coast is not in very good repair and it is wiser to return to Hillsborough the way we came.

Tours arranged from Grenada often include a trip to Sandy Island, to the south-west of Hillsborough. It is a popular spot for a day's outing and is enjoyed by the local inhabitants and by visitors alike. There is a good daytime anchorage and, with the reefs nearby, it is an excellent place for swimming and snorkelling, but spearfishing is prohibited.

Those with more time can visit the neighbouring islands of Petit St Vincent (PSV), Palm and Union. The first two are well-run holiday resorts, whereas the latter remains an unspoilt island much the same as Carriacou, but gradually becoming known as one of the few unspoilt areas left in the world.

Brief history

Very little is recorded of the early history of Carriacou and we have had to rely a great deal on church records to help us.

The original Carib name for this island was 'Kayryouacou', meaning 'land of reefs'. In the intervening years, the name lost a few vowels and changed a few consonants to arrive at the present spelling. It is believed that the first European inhabitants were French turtle fishermen who eventually cleared the land and planted crops. These were later joined by some of the inhabitants of Guadeloupe whose plantations on that island had been destroyed by some type of ant.

By the mid-eighteenth century, the British had taken possession of the island. In the late 1700s, cotton was the principal export and

A boat being built in the traditional Carriacou way (MICHAEL BOURNE)

sugar-cane, coffee, cocoa and indigo were also grown. At that time, the islands were easy prey for privateers of the many nations fighting for supremacy in these waters, and they would plunder and carry off whatever they could, including slaves. This was a very unsettling period for the peace-loving inhabitants.

Early in the nineteenth century, the British government handed over to the Anglican community (which was at that time the established church), all property that had previously been owned by the Roman Catholic Church. The Anglican rectors moved into a property near Windward and lived there for about half a century before transferring to Beauséjour, just outside Hillsborough.

In this period, a group of shipwrights arrived from Glasgow to build vessels for the planters, to transport the island's produce. This trade is continued by their descendants at Windward.

In 1886 there was a total eclipse of the sun and Father Stephen Joseph Perry SJ, from the Stonyhurst Observatory in the UK, came in company with another priest to observe the eclipse from Carriacou. They were rewarded with an excellent view of this phenomenon.

At that time the inhabitants were considered to be wretchedly poor, with most of the land being owned by absentee proprietors. By the early part of this century, the government solved this problem by purchasing estates, or parts of them, and instituting land settlement schemes. Later on, sons of the soil emigrated to Venezuela and Aruba to the oil refineries, to Panama for the building of the canal, to the United States and Britain for any jobs that they could find. They sent money home to their relatives, and this helped to bring a better standard of living to the people of the island. Those left at home also discovered what a lucrative trade there could be in the sale of uncustomed goods, and fishing and smuggling have been considered the principal occupations of the residents of Carriacou for many years. They are a very proud and independent people, great seamen and, unlike the black Grenadians, many families in Carriacou can proudly trace their ancestry back to the African tribe to which they belonged – the Ibo, the Yoruba, the Mandingo and others. Certain African customs are still practised, like the big drum. This tribal dance is executed only on special occasions, as at planting time in the early part of the year (the spring feasts), or the launching of a boat, or a tombstone feast, usually in the month of November when a tombstone is being erected on the grave of a relative; yet again, when someone has had a dream in which a dear departed has requested this ceremony. It begins with a huge feast (called a 'Buminay' – spelt phonetically as there is no known derivation of this word). The guests then form a circle in the centre of which the dancers will perform. The circle (or ring) is blessed with a sprinkling of jack iron (the local strong rum) then a sprinkling of water, repeated consecutively until the entire surface has been wet, the sprinklers gradually backing out of the ring. Then the drums begin and the dancers take over. It is a very moving ceremony and it is said that authentic African tribal dances are performed. The drums are usually made from barrels, over which goatskin is stretched taut. The drummer uses his fingers and palms to tap out the rhythm.

One of the most unforgettable and disastrous experiences occurred in July 1945 when a floating mine was washed ashore at Windward. With natural island curiosity, crowds soon gathered to see this strange sight. It is not known whether there was any tampering but unfortunately the mine did explode, killing nine people and injuring two.

Petite Martinique

Just about three miles from Windward in Carriacou is the island of Petite Martinique, settled by French fishermen about the same time as its sister isle. They also build their own boats for fishing and carry on a lucrative smuggling trade.

A story is told of an island commissioner stationed at Carriacou in the early 1930s who decided to clamp down severely on the smuggling. In view of this, he decided to pay a visit to Petite Martinique. When the islanders heard of his impending visit, they dug a huge hole in the sand and stuck a wooden cross at one end of it with the words 'The Grave of – – –' (naming the commissioner). It would seem that this little incident was too much for the poor man. The trade has continued unchecked despite several further attempts by various governments to quash it.

One very popular administrator was once handed a gift of two bottles of excellent French wine, and the islanders were very puzzled and upset when their kindness was, with regret, not accepted.

Petite Martinique is one of the many volcanic cones that abound in the islands of the Caribbean. From the top of the peak there is a splendid view of the other islands of the Grenadines, stretching as far as St Vincent.

| 11 |
At the end of the day

The sun is low in the sky and already the clouds are being painted with sunset colours: flame, salmon and peach fading to light pink. The artist at work this evening is superb. On the horizon the background sky of blue has paled, but the shading becomes deeper in the sweep of the arc, until right above us there is a brilliant blue against which the vermilion clouds move slowly, gradually changing

The last swim of the day (SINCLAIR)

shape and shade. Wisps of grey cloud float past, some edged with pink, with the more vivid colours resplendent in the sky behind them. There we have a Caribbean sunset; brilliant colours, forever changing, deepening, darkening. The light is beginning to fade as Mother Nature settles down. The birds become impatient and chattery as they gather to begin the flight to their resting places for the night. The last flock has gone to roost. The wind drops to a gentle breeze, and the waves that have been slapping the shore are more gentle now. No longer wild, they approach the land quietly, touch the sand on the beach, and pull away again like a ballet dancer swaying rhythmically to unheard music.

Everything is calm and peaceful. At the horizon the sun is beginning to dip into the sea. The final rays are brilliant, giving the clouds a last touch of fire before disappearing for the night. On a very clear evening, some people claim to see the famous green flash as the final tip of the sun disappears.

Sitting near the shore, we will suddenly discern movement around us. A number of land crabs have emerged from their holes in search of food. The slightest movement will cause them to disappear in a flash. If we sit quite still, we can watch one eating. There are two pincers at the front. The larger one at the right is used for breaking up the crab's food or for warding off an attack. The smaller pincer transports food to its mouth. It is fascinating to watch these interesting creatures.

Twilight is almost non-existent in the tropics. The sky is already darkening. The green fronds of the coconut palm have turned a deeper hue, then suddenly they are black shapes silhouetted against the paling sky.

Darkness has fallen, complete and utter. The fireflies begin their will-o-the-wisp dance all around us and the tiny whistling frogs start their song. The crickets join in with their shrill chirping. Now the bats are waking up to fly around in search of food. The different species in the island feed on insects, fish, nectar or fruit.

It is time for a 'sundowner' – a cocktail or some other favourite beverage. Gin or vodka taken with coconut water is a very popular drink, but the crème de la crème is our rum punch, which is so easy to make. Just remember this little ditty:

One of sour,/Two of sweet,/Three of strong,/Four of weak. Lime juice, syrup, rum and water. Mix together; pour on to crushed ice, top with a dash of Angostura bitters, some grated nutmeg, add a cherry and presto! Nectar, West Indian style! No doubt the gods quickly recognised the potency of this drink, which is hidden by the syrup.

Dinner can be an enjoyable and restful meal, where the day's activities are discussed and plans are made for tomorrow's excursions. Local dishes often feature on the menus of our hotels and restaurants but, for a completely local meal, well-prepared and beautifully served, a visit to La Belle Creole is recommended. This restaurant is run by the Hopkins brothers, who have carried on their parents' reputation for the preparation and serving of excellent native cuisine.

At Roydon's Guest House near to Grand Anse Beach, the wife of the owner offers demonstrations in local cooking, after which the guests can enjoy the meal prepared. This started as part of a package offered by a tour operator in the UK, but interested guests from any hotel would be welcome to join on any days that demonstrations are being given. This can easily be arranged through your hotel receptionist.

Meals with a difference are offered by Chinese and Italian restaurants. For the visitor who would like to sample local dishes there are a number of small eating places offering very basic but tasty meals. All of our hotels also include local foods in their menus. The visitor will find that we are inclined to use a lot of seasoning in our cooking.

After a lovely meal, we can relax with a cup of coffee or a drink, as we get ready for the evening's entertainment. One of the hotels might feature crab racing. Hermit crabs are placed in the centre of a ring, and bets are placed on which one will walk out of the ring first. Their shells are gently heated, then the crabs are released. Betting is usually fast and furious, and the crabs get much shouted encouragement as they make their way slowly and awkwardly to the finish line in many directions.

Steelband music is a popular form of entertainment as the performers can play all the popular tunes of the day as well as light classics and calypsos.

From time to time performances are staged at the Folk Theatre at Marryshow House (the School of Continuing Studies of the University of the West Indies). These shows can be very entertaining. There can

A dramatic sunset near Woburn *following pages* (ROGER BRATHWAITE)

be singing or dancing groups. Plays tend to have a West Indian flavour but they are well-written, well-directed and well-produced. The Trade Centre at Grand Anse is also used for performances.

A number of small nightclubs can be found in the hotel belt at the southern tip of the island as well as discos catering to the young and the young-at-heart.

of the fruit is coarser than that of the bluggoe and it did not become popular. These plants are now used mainly as shade for clonal cocoa. For many years the bluggoe has been a favourite diet food at the local hospitals for diabetics and pregnant women, particularly for its iron content. This tasty vegetable does not grace the tables of Trinidadians, who consider it only suitable to be fed to their animals!

Cocoa (Cacao)

The cacao trees are grown from seeds or from clones. From seedlings, the trees take about five years to bear. A clonal cacao tree on the other hand, bears in three to five years at which time it reaches its peak. Strangely enough, clonal cacao has been found to be not as high in fat content as that grown from seedlings.

The fruit, or pod, is oval shaped, and reddish brown or yellow. When cut open, the seeds are seen to be covered with a soft white substance which is quite pleasant to the taste. The seeds are extracted, washed, dried on huge trays in the sun, or in large bins electrically, then bagged for export to the more developed countries where it is processed into cocoa powder, chocolate and cocoa butter.

Cocoa is responsible for about 40% of our export earnings from agriculture.

Bamboo

Mention should also be made of the versatile bamboo plant of which we make very good use. The stems are cut at a joint and one end split into slivers and tied together to make a very useful broom, ideal for outdoor sweeping of paths and walkways. The stems are also used as handles for cocoa pickers, banana props and fishing rods.

Bamboo is used in the making of fish pots and baskets. In the past it was paramount in the building of wattle huts for the East Indian immigrants. A frame of bamboo poles was set up and interwoven with coconut fronds, plastered with a mixture of dung and clay. The thatched roofs were made from coconut fronds as well. Hardly any of these primitive huts remain on the islands. The bamboo is now being considered for the development of a craft industry.

A market is also a friendly meeting place *following pages* (SINCLAIR)

Flowers and trees

Although many exotic tropical blooms are grown on the island, only the anthurium is being considered on a commercial scale, as they can last as long as three weeks if cut in their prime. This aroid plant (of the arum family) is native to tropical America, and looks artificial. The long-stalked spadix is surrounded by a heart-shaped bract called the spathe. This beautifully formed waxen-looking bract is thick, and commonly a deep pink, but the colours range through pure white and several shades of orange, deep red and even green. This lily is used quite often in flower arrangements.

The bougainvillea is our national flower. The colours range through purples, reds, oranges to white. They bloom profusely in the dry season.

The several varieties of croton with their variegated leaves make beautiful hedges or garden shrubs. Other exotic blooms include the oleander, ginger lily, ixora, bird of paradise, frangipani, allamanda, hibiscus and poinsettia, whose leaves turn a flaming red at Christmas time. Several species of orchid are cultivated.

Beautiful tropical blossoms adorn the hillside, the valleys and our gardens. The red and yellow poui trees flower near the end of the dry season and create splashes of colour all over the island. These were originally planted as shade trees for the young cacao and nutmeg plants. The casuarina is a well-used windbreak. This plant grows very easily and is said to last for hundreds of years. Its long, drooping 'needles' give the impression of feathers swaying in the breeze. The yellow cassia is very pretty. The flaming red flamboyant graces many a lawn.

One of our most beautiful evergreens is the banyan. The silk cotton, another majestic tree, is one of our largest. During April and May, the seeds become windborne while still attached to a silky floss. Kapok, as the floss is known, is used to stuff cushions, pillows and toys.

Beautiful furniture is made from the mahogany and saman trees.

Of the food-producing trees, the coconut palm is the most versatile. The water from the mature nuts is very refreshing. The addition of gin or vodka produces a nectar fit for the gods. The dried nuts produce a white 'meat' which is grated and used in many dishes like oil down (with breadfruit), callaloo, and in cakes, pies and other desserts.

Cocoa pods on the tree *opposite* (SINCLAIR)

The copra can also be pressed for removal of the oil, and the residue is used as stock feed.

The coconut fronds are useful in thatching roofs and in the weaving of hats and bags. The fibre makes excellent door mats and is also used for stuffing mattresses. The air circulates more freely in a fibre mattress than in one made from any synthetic substance. The shell of the dried coconut is fashioned into all sorts of novelties.

The breadfruit tree is next in usefulness to our population. This was introduced to the West Indies from Tahiti in 1793 by Captain Bligh as a cheap source of food for the slave population. In an earlier attempt, the Captain's insistence on watering the young plants, at the expense of drinking water for his crew, resulted in the famous mutiny on his ship the *Bounty* in 1789. The breadfruit has a pale yellowish-green, warty-looking skin. The flesh is creamy white with a subtle, pleasant flavour when cooked.

Our fruit trees include the guava, sapodilla (a source of chicle for chewing gum), the mango, sugar apple, golden apple, pawpaw (papaya), mammee apple and soursop.

Cash crops

Some small farms have gone into the production of 'cash crops' for quicker returns. A large variety of vegetables is grown, for example cabbage, carrots, callaloo, beetroot, christophene, as well as seasoning peppers, chives, thyme and celery. Root vegetables consist of the yam, tannia, eddoe, dasheen and sweet potato. Some form of citrus fruit is available year round – sweet and Seville oranges, mandarins, grapefruit and limes.

The sea's bounty

Although our island is volcanic in origin, there are many coral reefs around our coasts and fish are plentiful. January to June is our heaviest fishing season when the catch includes tuna, kingfish, flying fish and dolphin. For those unfamiliar with our dolphin, it should be mentioned that this is actually a fish as opposed to the dolphin of the porpoise family which is a mammal, and which is well known to be man's friend in the sea. In Hawaii the dolphin fish is called Mahi Mahi.

January also begins the season for conch fishing. The conch is a tropical mollusc known locally as 'lambie'. The spiral shell is a pretty

The day's catch (MICHAEL BOURNE)

shape, about twelve inches long, with a shaded pink interior. It can be cleaned and used for all sorts of decoration in the house and garden. When held to the ear, the listener can hear what sounds like the murmuring of the sea. If properly cut, it serves as a useful trumpet, and this is how fishermen announce their arrival with a good catch for sale. The mollusc itself is stewed, soused, deep fried in batter or ground and made into rissoles or a pie. It has to be carefully prepared or it will be tough. Our restaurants serve very tasty lambie dishes which are recommended. The taste and texture is much like squid or octopus.

The rest of the year, by line fishing using the vertical method, catches of tuna (principally) as well as red hind, snapper, grouper and barracuda are made, while with seine fishing the haul will include jacks, round robin, couvalli and bonita. Naturally, the texture and the taste vary with the species, but they are all delicious. Jacks are the most popular fish. The large ones, about twelve inches or more in length, are a gourmet's delight when stuffed and baked. The smaller jacks, about two to three inches at the most, are fried crisp and eaten whole, bones and all.

Very little trawling is done, as the sharp edges of the coral on the reefs around the island would rip the nets to shreds.

In the last four months of the year, sea eggs and titiree are in season. Actually, the closed season for all shellfish is considered to be the months without the letter r – May, June, July and August. There are two types of sea urchin in these waters, each with a small globular body enclosed in a rigid spiny test. Locally, they are called black sea eggs and white sea eggs. The black variety is inedible. It has slender black spikes about four to six inches long. The tips break easily when touched, and remain embedded in the skin, causing discomfort and festering until the thorns are removed or they dissolve after some uncomfortable days. The local remedy is to pour some form of ammonia on the area as soon as possible; then the small black thorns rise to the surface of the skin and are easily removed.

The white sea urchin has smaller spines, about one inch long, and can easily be held as the spines are not as fragile. It is interesting to see the tiny spines moving back and forth in a live, freshly caught sea urchin. When cut open, ribbons of eggs are seen running along the inner casing of the shell. These are collected and used to fill whole, cleaned urchin cases. The filled shells are baked and sold. Cooks then remove the eggs, add some seasoning and a squeeze of lime juice, and fry lightly with garlic and onions.

Titiree (also called Teecheeree) are tiny silvery fish, not more than an inch and a half in length, which swarm up the rivers as 'whitebait'. They are strong swimmers and have been known to climb any vertical surface in their passage upstream. These are considered a culinary delicacy and are usually prepared in a batter and shallow fried.

Freshwater crayfish are caught in our rivers and streams. They resemble small lobsters and are much enjoyed in Grenada.

There are fish centres in a number of areas around the island where any surplus from the day's catch can be purchased and stored in cold rooms. Cooperatives are encouraged among the fishermen to help themselves in purchasing expensive fishing equipment. Foreign assistance has been received to aid in developing our fishing industry by way of soft loans through the International Fund for Agricultural Development (IFAD) as well as grants, donations and technical advice. Technical experts have come from Venezuela, sponsored by the Venezuela Investment Fund, who have been a big asset in training our fishermen in better methods for bigger catches.

Much assistance has also been received from Japan with a huge building project that has given us a jetty at Gouyave, a docking ramp at Victoria and a Styrofoam plant at True Blue, making large bins in which the fishermen can store their catch on ice. There is also a water supply facility for the fishermen at Calliste Bay. New fish centres have been constructed at Gouyave and Grenville, complete with offices, convention rooms and a modern refrigeration system for the storage of fish.

In St George's the new fishing complex at Melville Street is well under way. The storm surge in 1999 hampered progress a bit but work is now continuing apace. There will be a jetty for docking the boats as well as a large building complete with parking facilities. The lower storey will be used as a fish market, while the government's Fisheries Division will be housed upstairs. There will be two cold storage units and a modern ice making plant as well.

Grenada Commercial Fisheries Ltd, a government-run organisation is responsible for the buying and exporting of fish as well as supplies to the local market. This complex is located at Grand Mal, the building of which was also undertaken by the Japanese government.

|13|
Our spices

The nutmeg

Grenada's nutmeg is undoubtedly the most important spice produced on the island and is one of our three main export crops. It has the added distinction of being incorporated as an emblem in our national flag. Since the sixteenth century, the lucrative spice trade has been the cause of much piracy on the high seas, with many daring plots and feats to save or capture a fortune. In the Victorian era, nutmegs were very much in demand by the aristocracy. Ladies often wore a silver pendant especially designed to hold a nutmeg. This was worn around their necks at all times to ward off illness. A gentleman kept a nutmeg in a special case in his breast pocket for the same reason. Locally, it is used as a cure for colds, being grated on to a 'hot toddy' – a mixture of rum, lime and honey heated together and drunk as quickly as possible. It is also mixed with vaseline and rubbed on the chest, so that the pungent aroma can be breathed while asleep. Nutmeg oil is an ingredient in the well-known ointment 'Vicks Vaporub' popularly used in this hemisphere for the relief of congestion caused by colds.

Plants of the nutmeg tree arrived in Grenada in 1843. A popular legend has it that the plants were imported by a doctor who had spent some time in the East Indies and enjoyed the aroma and flavour of the nutmeg, which he knew would improve the taste of his favourite Planter's Punch. Another legend is that they were brought here by a Mr Cantin, but we do know that the first trees were planted at Penang estate in the parish of St Andrew. The trees thrived in this beautiful climate and rich soil, and over the years the crop developed into a thriving export trade. The nutmeg tree is a tropical evergreen that can grow to a height of sixty feet. It likes rich soil which is well watered and well drained. A popular belief is that it grows better if it can smell the salt from the sea. It bears fully in about eight years, with a steady increase in yield each year. The crop is continuous year-round, with heavier yields during the months of February to April and August to October.

This nutmeg is nearly ready to fall (SINCLAIR)

Grenada's nutmegs are much sought after, as the nuts are considered to be of a very high quality. It is interesting to note that weeds will not grow under a nutmeg tree. The fruit itself is round and yellow, not unlike an apricot. When mature, this splits in half and a dark brown shell can be seen, covered by a vivid red lacy-looking membrane (or aril). This is the mace which is highly prized in the pharmaceutical industry, apart from being looked upon by the adventurous cook as a necessary addition to cakes, pies and sauces. The fruit is never picked from the tree, but the nut is allowed to fall to the ground. If left for any time it would rot, so it is gathered immediately and the red mace stripped from the shell and dried separately. In 1947 farmers in Grenada got together and formed a cooperative – the Grenada Cooperative Nutmeg Association (GCNA) which is now the sole exporter of nutmegs and mace on the island. In the GCNA processing stations, the mace is dried to a light orange colour and sorted ready for shipment. The nutmegs are sold in the shell, or cracked and sorted prior to shipment. If the shell has not been cracked, the nutmeg inside can remain fresh for a long time. A new nutmeg reconditioning plant is now in operation to take care of the processing of nutmegs principally for the American market. Grated nutmeg is a popular addition to the famous rum punch, or eggnog and other beverages. It is also used in the making of jams, jellies and syrup. The nutmeg is also much sought after in the perfume industry and as a preservative.

Nutmegs and mace together account for a large portion of the island's revenue from export crops. Over the years markets have been lost and regained, prices have fallen and risen. At the moment, Grenada is receiving a good price on the world markets for this export crop and a record EC$10m was paid to farmers in December 1999 over and above the original purchase price. A further EC$3m was distributed in April 2000 and in December of the same year another EC$10m will be divided among the happy farmers.

A distillation plant for the production of nutmeg oil has been constructed at Marli in St Patrick's. Mace oil is also being produced. These are both used for medicinal purposes and are becoming a rising export product.

There are several processing stations around the island, and the pleasant smell of the spice can lure anyone into paying them a visit. The station at Gouyave is well worth a visit when touring the west coast.

Many additional spices are grown on the island, and small amounts are exported from time to time by the Minor Spices Society. When you explore the town of St George's with the aid of this guide, you will be able to find your way to their office, if the pleasant rich scent of spice has not led you there on its own! Here's a brief account of our other spices:

Allspice (Jamaica pepper)
This is the dried berry of the pimento tree, and is supposed to taste like a combination of cinnamon, clove and nutmeg, hence the name.

Estate workers separating mace from the nutmeg (SINCLAIR)

The tree is native to the Caribbean and the green fruit, about the size of a small pea, changes to dark brown when picked and dried in the sun. It can be used as a pickling spice, whole or ground, or for flavouring wines or meat dishes. It is also added to gravies, sauces, relishes, preserves, mincemeat, puddings, cakes and beverages, and sometimes even used to hide the taste of medicines. Ground allspice can be found in many spice mixtures, including curry powder.

The bay leaf

This is the aromatic leaf of an evergreen tree of the laurel family. In Grenada the leaves are sold green or dried, and used in soups, meat dishes and pickles. They particularly enhance all tomato dishes. Always be careful to ensure that the leaf is taken out before any dish is served, as the spine of the leaf can be dangerous if swallowed by accident. Bay rum is made from diluted alcohol and oil of bay, which is distilled from the leaves. This is much used in the sick room to cool fevers, etc.

Black pepper

These begin life as red berries about the size of peas, growing on a vine. They are wrinkled and black when dried, and are familiarly known as 'peppercorns'. They are used either whole for pickling, or ground in meat and vegetable dishes, gravies, etc. Pepper mills grace many tables where owners enjoy the taste of freshly ground pepper on their food. The vine produces two crops a year.

Chili or bird pepper

This is a small, very hot red pepper about the length of a phalanx of the little finger and about a quarter of its width. It is very popular with birds, who eat them whole. It is not so popular with humans, who are forced to show more respect for this hot spice.

Cinnamon

This is another evergreen tree and like the bay, also related to the laurel family. The bark is carefully peeled off and often rolled into 'sticks' before being dried. Whole or ground, the dried bark has a sweet delicate aroma and is a much liked addition to cakes, breads, biscuits, puddings and stewed fruit. It is delicious on broiled grapefruit, sautéed or baked bananas, or any apple or pineapple dishes. Oil of cinnamon is used in various flavourings and sweets.

Clove

Cloves are the dried, unopened flower buds of a tree that can grow to a height of 40 feet. The flower buds are first a pale green, growing darker and changing to a deep red. These are picked and dried to a dark brown colour. Cloves have a pungent aroma and are said to relieve toothache and nausea. They can be purchased whole or ground and are used whole for decorating legs of ham and pork. Cloves can be used for flavouring meat dishes, gravies, cakes, puddings and fruit beverages and are also an ingredient in some pickles and preserves. The oil of cloves, distilled from the buds, is added to some liqueurs and perfumes.

Ginger

This is a plant with a leafy, reed-like stem. The root is the spice. Dried and ground, it is used as a flavouring in cakes, breads and drinks. Most of us are familiar with gingerbread and ginger beer. Oil of ginger is said to allay pain.

Sapote

This is a large tree with brown, rough-surfaced fruit. The flesh is orange-red and edible, with a rich, cloying taste. It is used for making preserves and beverages. The large seed has three sides. Two of them look like old polished mahogany, while the third is a lighter brown, and rough. The kernel is creamy white and has an almond flavour. It is grated and used in cakes, pies, etc.

Tonka bean

From a large tree, the fibrous pods have a very dark brown seed with a strong fragrance. Soaked in alcohol, it is sometimes used in place of vanilla. It is the source of coumarin which is used in perfumes and flavourings, and as an anti-coagulant.

Turmeric

This is locally known as saffron. It resembles the ginger-root, except that it has a rich orange-yellow colour. The true saffron comes from the dried stigmas of a plant, whereas this is a root. It is an ingredient of curry powder and also gives the yellow colour to prepared mustard. Turmeric is also used as a dye, and to flavour and colour breads, meats, rice and some medicines. White paper soaked in turmeric is used by chemists to detect the presence of alkalis. It is called curcuma or turmeric paper.

Vanilla

The vanilla plant bears orchid-like flowers, the long brown pod being the vanilla bean which is used in flavouring all sorts of sweet dishes and cakes after being distilled. It is also employed in the perfume industry.

Locally, teas are brewed from many of these spices to help relieve different ailments like chest and stomach aches, or colds and fever.

|14|
Our birds and animal life

Most visitors expect to see all our birds as brilliantly coloured as are our flowers, but regrettably this is not so. The magnificent plumage of the macaw or the scarlet ibis can be enjoyed in neighbouring Trinidad or in tropical South America, but they have never travelled as far north as Grenada.

Our birds belong mainly to the tropical North American group. Parrots were recorded as being in Grenada and Carriacou in the sixteenth and seventeenth centuries but they no longer exist here. It is suspected that the introduction of the Mona monkey had much to do with their demise.

For ornithologists and those interested in making an in-depth study of our bird life, Father Raymund P. Devas has written a very interesting and informative booklet entitled *Birds of Grenada, St Vincent and the Grenadines* which can be obtained at our local library. Dr J. R. Groome also, in *A Natural History of the Island of Grenada*, lists the birds found here, with their scientific names. There are several other reference books written on the birds of the West Indies which will include all the species found on this island.

A great many of the birds seen are winter migrants from the north, but we do have a number of resident species which will be mentioned here.

The hummingbird is a tiny, beautiful bird about four to five inches long. It has brilliant iridescent plumage, very powerful wings, and a long slender bill made especially for gathering the insects and nectar from flowers. The three most common are the emerald-throated hummingbird, the Antillean crested hummingbird and the doctor bird.

A number of swifts are also present in the mountain regions, the one most often seen being the lesser Antillean swift (mountain swift).

Many of our swallows are migrants, being seen mostly between February and August, but even as late as November. They appear to frequent different parts of the island at different times of the year. The species most prevalent is the purple martin.

Flycatchers (pippiree) are generally seen all over the island, the top-knot pippiree being quite common.

Only one species of the wren family lives here. The southern house wren is seen nesting in houses in April and again in August. Of the thrasher family we have the southern mockingbird. The yellow-eyed thrush or grieve has a rich, melodious song which can be heard morning and evening. Other species of thrush are seen, but more rarely.

There are two families of birds generally known as see-see birds in Grenada. These include the yellow see-see or sucrier, and the black see-see. The second family are finches, like the blue-black see-see or prezeet (blue-black grassquit), the black-faced grassquit, the lesser Antillean bullfinch or red-throat see-see and the yellow-bellied seed-eater or white-beak see-see.

Our blackbirds are about ten or eleven inches long. They go about in pairs and sometimes in quite large flocks. They are often seen on the backs of cattle and sheep picking at ticks.

The soursop bird or Antillea calliste is very common. The cuckoo-manioc or rain bird emits a curious guttural sound which it is claimed is calling for rain, hence the nickname.

The smooth-billed ani or tick birds (corbeau) live in communities and have one very large nest. The hens take it in turns to sit on the eggs, which are sometimes as many as twenty-one to a nest.

We boast of one owl – the lesser Antillean barn owl or jumbie bird. There are a number of hawks: the chicken hawk or gree-gree; the fish hawk or osprey; the sparrow hawk or American kestrel, and a number of migrant hawks. Of the dove family, the ramier is our largest game bird. Other common doves are the Trinidad ground dove, the seaside dove or wild pigeon, a small ground dove, the Grenada dove – a rare species peculiar to the island, and a rarer mountain dove.

A number of water birds frequent our lakes and bays and, more often, the small uninhabited islands around our coast.

The belted kingfisher is a common winter resident in the West Indies, and can be seen between September and April at La Sagesse Bay, Levera Lake and Green Island.

The water-hen, also known as Florida gallinule or red-seal coot is common at Levera Lake and the lagoon at Simon.

The Caribbean coot is found in quantity around Lake Antoine and Levera Pond. Wilson's plover and the semi-palmated plover are both common. Snipe and sandpipers are winter migrants from the north.

A few ducks can be seen around the fresh water lakes in the north of the island, the ruddy duck or blue-bill being the most regularly spotted. Migrants from the northern winter include the mallard, green-winged teal and blue-winged teal.

The pied-billed grebe is often seen around Levera Pond. The heron family is also well represented with the gaulin or little blue heron, the little crabier or little green heron, and the yellow-crowned night heron or crabier. The cattle egret has become a resident breeding species and can be seen all over the island.

Most of our sea birds can be seen from the shore, but a few are found only far out to sea, or on isolated islets and rocks.

The laughing gull or mauve is our only seagull. Then there are the gull-billed tern, the roseate tern or careete (pronounced caweete), the bridled tern, the noddy tern or mwen, Audubon's shearwater, the brown pelican, the brown booby, the white booby and the red-footed booby.

The man-of-war or frigate bird is seen all over Grenada's coastline, often soaring to a great height. It seldom catches its own fish, although it can do so with its claws as well as with its bill. It prefers to fight other birds for their catch. It enjoys playing with a caught fish which it will drop from a height then swoop down to catch again before the fish reaches the water.

Of the tropical birds, we can lay claim to having two of the three species which are said to be in the entire world.

Animal life

The Mona monkey is our largest wild animal. It is of West African origin, and was probably introduced during the years of slave trading. A fully grown male can weigh as much as 56 pounds. They live in the mountain forests and are popular game for local hunters.

The mouse opossum or manicou gros-yeux is reddish-brown and about the size of a rat. It has large, bulging eyes and a prehensile tail which is used for transporting its bedding material as well as for climbing. The big toe of its hind foot is opposable like a thumb. On the other hand, the large opossum or manicou is a scavenger and, being omnivorous, is a pest to poultry and wild birds.

The nine-banded armadillo or tatou lives largely in the forested areas of the island. It has strong, horny plates over most of its body and is hunted for food. It lives mainly on termites and other insects, on worms, lizards, roots and fruit, feeding mostly at night. It is interesting to note that the young in each litter are always of one sex.

In Grenada, eleven different species of bat, of varying sizes, have been identified. We are fortunate, however, to be free of the vampire bat which is known as a carrier of paralytic rabies on the South American mainland.

The agouti or 'gouti' became extinct by over-hunting for food and sport, and destruction by the mongoose. Some years ago it was reintroduced into the island from Trinidad and hopefully is becoming established once again. The only indigenous rodent, it is a long-legged, agile creature with hoof-like claws, and is valued for its meat.

The Burmese mongoose was imported from Jamaica about 1870 to control rats in the cane belt. It is now a great pest, hunting by day and destroying poultry, lizards and other small animals.

There are any number of the lizard family which are all harmless. The iguana or 'guana' is our largest lizard, reaching a length of over five feet. It has a greyish-green body and a long tail which can be used quite effectively as a whip in self-defence. It swims well in the sea, and is a good climber. A meal of the flesh of this lizard is considered locally to be a choice feast.

A large green turtle (MICHAEL BOURNE)

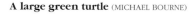

We have no venomous snakes.

The white-headed worm snake is small, with a body the colour of polished mahogany. The tree boa is fairly common, growing to a length of about six feet. It is an excellent rat-catcher. Its colour varies from marbled greens, purples and browns to near red. The tree snake or grass snake is a small, greenish-brown snake. The cribo, a constrictor, is larger and the colour of slate. It is very good at keeping our rodent population under control.

All turtles and their eggs are food delicacies and much in demand. As a consequence they are given protection by law from 1st May to 30th September each year. There is also a minimum legal weight of 25 pounds for turtles. The green turtle is caught chiefly for its meat, deriving its name from the green colour of its fat. A four-foot specimen can weigh as much as 500 pounds.

The scales or plates on the back of the hawksbill turtle supply the raw material for tortoise shell from which many ornamental items can be made. These have now become an endangered species and are fully protected.

The loggerhead turtle is also caught here for food but the flesh is inferior to the previous two.

The humpback whale used to be hunted from a small station at Glover's Island until about 1927, and appears to have been almost exterminated in this area. The occasional one can still be seen from time to time on its migration northwards.

The pilot whale or 'blackfish' is still hunted, in a primitive manner, in the Grenadine Islands.

|15|
Our sports and festivals

Football (soccer) is the most popular sport in Grenada, and is considered our national sport. Every boys' secondary school on the island has a team, and the younger boys in the junior schools are often seen practising with any type of ball that they can procure. Most clubs are registered with the Grenada Football Association (GFA) which arranges football competitions annually between the premier league and first and second division teams. There is also an NCB knockout and a Heineken League competition, an inter-parish senior competition and an under-sixteen team competition. These are all sponsored by local firms and the Ministry of Sport. The official football season is from May to December each year.

Our cricket season lasts from late December to May. Interschool matches are regularly featured and the English-speaking Caribbean, from Jamaica to Guyana, takes part in tournaments from which players are selected to represent the West Indies in international matches.

Basketball has its share of devoted fans. Local tournaments are held annually. Some years ago, one member of the Basketball Association was awarded a scholarship to an American university for his outstanding performance in this field.

Netball, badminton, volley-ball and table tennis are played, but neither baseball nor American football has caught on here at present.

Tennis has become quite popular among the youth. The Grenada Tennis Association in conjunction with the Ministry of Youth and Sport, gives all sorts of encouragement to the youngsters who may one day be in a position to represent their country in international competitions. A school tennis initiative programme has been introduced in many of the schools and three junior tournaments are held in the island each year. The first takes place at the end of January; the Coca-Cola championship is held in July, and the final tournament comes off in December. In 1991 a young Grenadian was selected as a member of the OECS Davis Cup team. In the last three years other young Grenadians have had a similar honour.

Windsurfing at Grand Anse (GRENADA TOURIST BOARD)

Of the wider Caribbean junior tournaments that are held annually, Grenada usually competes for the Barclays Bank trophy in Barbados at Easter. The IBM IBIS International Junior Tennis Championship comes round in August. The ITF (14 and under) Caribbean Development Championship also draws some eager contestants. Recently, Grenada came fifth out of twelve contestants, tying with the Virgin Islands.

Grenada also participates in the CAC Games, the Carifta Games, the Pan American Games, and since 1984 we have also participated in the Olympics. This year we sent a team to participate in the track and field events and in swimming.

The Richmond Hill Tennis Club is a private membership club which welcomes interested visitors, and use of the courts can easily be arranged for a small fee. Temporary membership would be required for anyone staying in the island for over three months. The bar is open daily from 3.00 p.m. closing when the last member leaves – usually between 6.30 and 8.00 p.m. The Tanteen tennis courts are also available to visitors and some of the hotels have courts of their own.

The Grenada Yacht Club, another private membership club, is open every day from 10.00 a.m. to 8.30 p.m. to its members and visiting yachtsmen and women. Drinks and light snacks can be purchased as well as a pleasant lunch every day except Sunday. Occasionally there is a 'happy hour' when drinks are served at reduced prices in the late afternoon. Members and duly introduced visitors are welcome.

Docking facilities are available at reasonable rates. The club is in the process of extending their jetty by a further 180 feet. Yacht races are organised for almost every month in the year, ending at different venues like True Blue Resort or La Source at Point Salines, or back at the club where there will be eating and drinking and much merriment to mark the close of the races and the celebration of the winners. The 'end of hurricane season' race seems to be the most popular as yachtsmen and women gather to celebrate the passing of yet another hurricane season.

A junior sailing programme is normally scheduled each year when the children of members and other youngsters in the community are taught the rudiments of sailing.

The Spice Island Bill Fish Tournament, a modified tag and release sports fishing tournament, takes place during the third week in January every year. This tournament started in 1964 and has become very popular. Participating boats come from Trinidad, St Lucia, Barbados, Martinique and even as far away as the USA. The anglers look for blue marlin, white marlin and sailfish most of which are photographed then tagged and returned to the deep.

At the Easter weekend, there is a small regatta at Petite Martinique, usually involving boats from the neighbouring Grenadine islands – a fun weekend for all.

In June, a Spice Jazz Festival takes place and jazz lovers from all the islands gather to enjoy a wonderful weekend of performances.

At all the marinas, yachts can be chartered for a day's cruising, a weekend, a week or as long as you like! The crews are efficient and very knowledgeable about Grenada and the Grenadines. Arrangements for various types of water sports may be made at Grand

Carnival time *following pages* (JIM RUDIN)

Anse beach near to the Spice Island Inn. Sunfish, catamarans and speed boats can be rented. You can enjoy water-skiing, a day's snorkelling around our many fascinating coral reefs, scuba diving, deep-sea fishing or just a nice relaxing sail.

There are two shipwrecks that will be of interest to divers. The *SS Orinoco* was wrecked off the rocks at La Sagesse Point in St David's in 1900. Here's how it happened. Grenadians have always been very religious, and on 1st November each year, a holy day on the church calendar, it was the practice to light candles on the graves of the dear departed. This is an impressive sight as thousands of candles are lit and the living visit with each other at the place of the dead. Electricity had not yet come to the island, and the ship mistook the myriads of lights at the St David's cemetery for the town of St George's, thus coming to grief on the rocks. The waters on this Atlantic side of the coast are rough, and only experienced divers should attempt to explore this wreck.

On the other hand, the *Bianca C*, which caught fire and sank in the outer harbour of St George's, is in calmer waters with visibility sometimes up to 200 feet. Exploring this wreck can be an exciting experience.

Our golf course is considered one of the best natural nine-hole courses in the West Indies. The Grenada Golf and Country Club welcomes interested visitors who are allowed the facilities of the club for a small fee. Members compete for a monthly medal. The club's bar is open daily from 8.00 a.m. to 6.00 p.m. to members and bona fide visitors.

Festivals

Carnival is our largest annual festival. This celebration originally took place only in countries where Roman Catholicism was the dominant religion and was a two-day 'spree' encouraged by the Church. At this time people sing, dance and make merry, to rid themselves of the sins of the flesh just prior to the observance of the Lenten season with its forty days of abstinence and fasting, when good Christians try to improve the quality of their lives. With the march of progress the religious significance is not as strong. The celebration has been adopted by many other West Indian islands at different times of the year, thus ruling out the original meaning of the festival. In the recent past our Carnival celebrations were shifted to the month of August.

134

Preparations normally begin months in advance, and from the week before Carnival competitions are held for the Junior King and Queen and the Calypso King. On the Friday before Carnival, Panorama (the steelband competition) is staged. On Saturday night, the Carnival Queen is chosen from a field of contestants sponsored by island business places. These competitions are held at Queen's Park and visitors to the island are often invited to join local judges in making their decisions. The Carnival Queen contestants parade in costume and in evening dress and the enthusiastic crowd makes its wishes known by loud cheers or boos. We are also entertained with calypsos and other performances which make for a very enjoyable evening. In the sister isle of Carriacou however, it is still upheld in the two days before Lent.

Sunday is Dimanche Gras, when the King and Queen of the bands are chosen. That night, dances are held island-wide, often continuing until Jour Ouvert, now called J'ouvert (pronounced jou-vay) 'the beginning of the day'. People take to the streets in all sorts of ridiculous garb, often satirical, relating to incidents which have occurred during the past year. There can be much wit and humour in these presentations. Few steelbands turn out, and sometimes the revellers have just two bits of iron or steel banging together to a rhythmic beat.

Normally by eight in the morning everybody is off the streets until about midday when lovely costumes begin to appear as the bands gather at pre-arranged spots for their journey to Queen's Park to take part in the pageant, again before a huge audience. These bands can be anything from 20 to 500 strong, depicting whatever the imagination can devise in the firmament and on earth. We see angels, planets and stars, satellites, birds, animals, fish, underwater scenes, folklore, colourful historical events, all gorgeously portrayed. In the evening, the fête (local parlance for a party) continues island-wide.

The morning of Shrove Tuesday begins quietly enough as the revellers try to recover from the night of drinking and debauchery. Again at midday, groups of costumed revellers begin to assemble at specified points and the Parade of the Bands begins around the streets of St George's. Many of the bands have steelbands with them, beating out their favourite calypso of the season. The most popular one becomes the Road March of that year. It can be a spectacular sight enjoyed by participants and onlookers alike, with everybody jumping and shuffling to the irresistible rhythm of the calypso.

The steelband conveys the music and rhythm of the Caribbean (JIM RUDIN)

The steelband is an art form that developed in Trinidad in the late 1930s. West Indians are all very musical and Trinidadians, in particular, have always enjoyed a good fête with lots of singing and dancing. It is not uncommon at a gathering for someone to start a song, with everyone soon joining in. To keep the rhythm, an impromptu band will be formed with pot covers, rubbish bins and bottles, all being struck with sticks or knives in time to the tunes. The steelband developed from this early beginning. It was found that dents in pans produced different sounds, and that oil drums, which were plentiful in the oil industry there, were ideal for hammering into shapes that produced certain musical notes. The pans are cut to different depths and this gives the required pitch. The entire drum, with one end removed, is used to obtain the bass notes, and the shallowest pans give the treble notes. The highest pitch is produced by the tenor pan, known as the ping pong. The sticks with which these pans are beaten are covered with stretched rubber to get the correct resonance.

Pan, the music of the steelband, soon became a popular form of music, particularly at Carnival time when the pan men would jump in the streets with the light pans hanging from a strap around their necks. When the bass pans were introduced, an easier mode of transport had to be devised and stands were made on wheels so that they could be pulled along easily. Apart from calypsos, many familiar songs and classical tunes can be played, but few pan men are able to read music and must rely strictly on their ear. Finally, this music was so well accepted that competitions were included at Carnival to choose the best steelband each year. This competition became known as 'Panorama'.

With the islands so close, a matter of ninety miles apart, pan music soon came to Grenada. In the early 1940s small groups were formed, the first band probably originating in Belmont. This was followed by Hell's Cats, formed in St John Street in the city. Each band had to be called something special, and unique names were devised. The 1950s saw larger bands like 'GASPO' (Grenada All-Steel Percussion Orchestra) which was led by Bert Marryshow, a son of our famous politician, T. Albert Marryshow. At about the same time, the Emmanuel brothers, who lived in Cox Alley in St George's, also formed a group which became known as the 'Coxipaters'. A group from Morne Jaloux chose 'The Katzenjammer Kids' as their title.

As we also celebrate Carnival in Grenada, Panorama became an important part of the competitions here as well. Over the years, many steelbands broke up as new ones were formed. It is interesting to note that the Coxipaters are still in existence, but now under the name of Angel Harps, one of our leading steelbands. In 1977 they made their first recording which was titled 'As Prescribed'. This was a collection of popular calypsos and other tunes, and became a big hit locally.

Catchy names are chosen for our bands. In the parish of St George there are the Angel Harps, Coca-Cola Pan Wizards, New Dimensions, Pan Lovers and the Comancheros. In St Mark's we find Cap Bank Syncopaters and in St Andrew's there is the Grenlec Rainbow City All-Stars. These bands often perform at the various hotels for the enjoyment of our visitors. Tuning the pans is a very specialised field and there are few people locally who have become proficient at this. It is long, tedious work as the tops of the pans have to be hammered down, or sunk, to stretch the metal. Then the notes on the pans are marked out, then ponged up: that is, the note sections are raised slightly by hitting the inside of the top of the pan. Next, the pan is heated thoroughly before the tuning begins, carefully, note by note being tapped until the correct pitch is obtained. For many years this was done strictly by ear, but now there are electronic devices to assist the tuner. For about ten years in the 1970s we had a national tuner by the name of Wilfred Harris. He now works from the Bahamas, but still comes back every year to assist the bands at Carnival time. Tuners also come from Trinidad to assist us at this important time.

Each band has to have an arranger for adapting the music for playing on pans. These arrangers are often the only people who know anything about reading musical scores, but there are still some excellent arrangers who are unable to read a score, and depend entirely on inborn musical ability and a good ear.

The steelband is now included in the curriculum of many schools in Grenada.

At first the steelband was heard only at Carnival each year and never, ever, during the Lenten season. Now that this form of music has become more acceptable, we can have this entertainment year-round.

The calypso is the music of the island. This type of satirical ballad also originated in Trinidad and very quickly became popular in the other West Indian islands, and even further abroad. The tunes are catchy and the verses usually portray a topical story told with great wit and humour. Calypsonians always choose outlandish names for themselves like 'Kootsman' and 'Scrunter'. One of the greatest of these, 'Sparrow', was born in Grenada, but grew up in Trinidad and became world famous as a great calypso composer and singer.

On 7th February each year, we celebrate the attainment of our Independence from British rule in 1974. There are services in the churches followed by a parade, usually held at the Queen's Park.

May 1st is celebrated as Labour Day. A procession of all active unions is held annually, each year at a different venue throughout the island.

Corpus Christi is a Roman Catholic festival which takes place on the Thursday after Trinity Sunday (a moveable feast, eight weeks after Easter). The RC community celebrates this day with a procession through the streets of each town.

With the ecumenical movement sweeping the world, the Anglican community joins in this celebration in Grenada. Conversely, the Feast of St George is a Patronal Festival of the Anglican Church and is celebrated on St George's Day, or the nearest Sunday to it. Other Christian denominations are invited to take part in the procession through the town of St George's.

Fisherman's Birthday is another Roman Catholic festival that is celebrated each year on 29th June, the feast of St Peter and St Paul. Church services are held in every parish on the island, the fishermen's boats and nets are blessed, and there is eating, drinking and merrymaking for the rest of the day. The largest fête takes place at the fishing town of Gouyave, where boat races are organised and the festivities continue with music and dancing in the streets until the small hours of the morning. The 23rd April is considered the birthday of the town of St George's and its 300th anniversary was celebrated in the year 2000. This will now be incorporated as St George's Day with a special commemoration being held every year.

Our most recent celebration is 25th October which is called Thanksgiving Day. On this day in 1983 at the request of our Governor General, the Organisation of Eastern Caribbean States, with great assistance from the United States of America, freed the island from the threat of communism.

The big annual event at Carriacou is the August Regatta. The first Monday in August is always a holiday in memory of the emancipation from slavery. The day after is also a public holiday, given us early in this century by the Legislative Council of the day who were all keen on horse-racing. At that time, meetings were held in early January, at Easter and in August when an extra day was tagged on to an existing holiday so that prominent business people could enjoy their races. Horse-racing is a thing of the past, but some of the holidays remain. The Carriacou Regatta involves mostly work boats, but yachts also participate in the various events. Participants and holiday-makers converge from all the neighbouring islands. The larger pleasure yachts also make for Carriacou at this time of the year for an exciting weekend of sailing, drinking and dancing. In Grenville a Rainbow City Festival is held also on the first weekend in August. Various contests take place and there are stage performances as well as displays of local handicraft. The streets are alive with revellers. There is much dancing and merrymaking, with steelbands beating out popular tunes. Numerous makeshift stalls on the pavements offer delectable items for sale and much fun is had by all. Fête for so!

In the field of art

There are two outstanding local playwrights who produce plays regularly, mostly dealing with local topics, but written in such a way that strangers can usually follow and enjoy the shows. These are performed either at Marryshow House which is the Centre for Continuing Studies of the University of the West Indies, or at the Government Trade Centre building at Grand Anse. Sometimes the country districts benefit from a performance as well. There are some experienced actors who give excellent performances.

A number of local artists and sculptors have their work exhibited annually at a special Arts Festival held in the early part of each year.

Local choirs and dance groups perform regularly at our hotels as well as at other functions. Grenadians on the whole have a great ear for music, and love to sing and dance, much to the enjoyment of our visitors.

| 16 |
The way we cook

One of our civil servants had the opportunity to be chosen for specialised training in the United Kingdom some years ago, where he acquitted himself admirably. On his return to the island he was asked, among other things, how he had enjoyed the English cooking.

'Not at all,' was the reply. 'They don't season their food at all, and every day with lunch and dinner they serve potato, potato, potato until I was sick of it. In Grenada I am accustomed to a choice of so many vegetables like yam, dasheen, tannia, eddoes, sweet potato, breadfruit and bluggoes. I cannot understand how those people could like that potato so much!'

It is true that we have a great many starchy vegetables. They can be peeled, boiled, sliced and served with a dot of butter, or crushed with milk and egg, then sprinkled with breadcrumbs and baked, or fried in small 'cakes'. Bluggoes, breadfruit and eddoes are nice

A large Grenadian lobster (langouste) (GRENADA TOURIST BOARD)

'soused' – the hot cooked vegetable is sliced into a mixture of lime juice, water, salt, onions and pepper.

Some green vegetables and fruit will also be new to the visitor and we can assure you that much pleasure awaits anyone willing to explore these exciting new gastronomic experiences. We use a lot of hot sauce made with minced hot peppers and vinegar. It is added during cooking and included in the condiments served at table as well. This extremely hot sauce should be approached with caution! Several tropical vegetables and fruit are now available in North American and European markets. A number of recipes are included in this chapter to encourage further exploration into a new world of taste. All measurements are given in imperial, with metric and American measures included.

We shall begin with a beverage. Ginger beer used to be given to the slaves on the estates as a celebration drink in place of hard liquor. This has become a popular drink, particularly at Christmas time.

Ginger beer

2 ozs (50 g) [½ cup] powdered ginger	1 gallon (4 l) [20 cups] boiling water
2 ozs (50 g) [½ cup] cream of tartar	½ teaspoon active dry yeast
Juice and rind of 2 small limes	1½ lbs (700 g) [3 cups] sugar

In a large jar, add boiling water to ginger, limes and cream of tartar. Stir thoroughly and cover. When lukewarm, stir in yeast dissolved in 2 tablespoons lukewarm water with ¼ teaspoon sugar. Stir well, cover and let stand for about six hours. Strain carefully through a muslin. Sweeten with the sugar, bottle and refrigerate.

Callaloo (callilu) is the large green leaf of the dasheen plant. It is rich in iron and vitamins and is our local spinach. As a vegetable it is cooked with salt beef or pigs' tails. The addition of coconut milk gives a subtlety to the dish. As a soup, local land crabs are often added to produce a unique and interesting flavour.

Crab and callaloo soup

4 oz (100 g) [¼ lb] salt beef
1 dozen dasheen leaves
  (about 12 oz) (350 g) [¾ lb]
6 okras
1 onion, diced
1 clove garlic, crushed
1 chive
1 sprig thyme

2 pints (1 l) [5 cups] boiling
  water
4 oz (100 g) [¼ lb] cooked
  crabmeat
2 tablespoons (2 T) [3 T]
  vinegar
1 tablespoon (1 T) [1½ T] butter

Salt and pepper to taste

Soak salt beef for about half an hour. Cut in small pieces. Wash dasheen leaves; strip stalks and midribs and cut up leaves. Wash okras. Top and tail them and cut them in small slices. Add first six ingredients to boiling water. Reduce heat and simmer gently until everything is soft. Add crab meat and vinegar and simmer for five minutes longer. Add butter. Adjust seasoning. This soup can be strained, liquidised, or left as is, depending on preference. It is even nicer if left for about half an hour for the flavours to intermingle. Then re-heat gently and serve. Grenadians clean and cook the local land crabs, then add the body, legs and pincers to the soup so that the family can enjoy cracking the shells and extracting the delicious meat.

Jackfish or jacks are one of the most popular fish, particularly when stuffed and baked.

Stuffed jacks

For this the large jacks are used. Clean and bone the fish. Using a sharp knife, slit along each side of the backbone and remove it carefully. Season with chive and thyme, lime juice and a little salt, and allow to marinate. Meanwhile prepare a bread stuffing. Fill the cavity carefully. Fasten with toothpicks or skewers. The fish can be floured and fried in hot fat, or if preferred, dot with butter, cover with foil and bake for about 25 to 30 minutes in a moderate oven (350°F) until flaky. Uncover for the last five minutes to brown nicely. Nice with a parsley sauce.

Cornmeal recipes were brought over from Africa with the slave population, and remain a popular food.

Corn cou-cou (coo-coo)

6 oz (175 g) [$\frac{3}{4}$ cup] cornmeal
$\frac{1}{2}$ pint (3 dl) [$1\frac{1}{4}$ cups] water (or coconut milk)
1 teaspoon salt
1 tablespoon butter (or 2   1 small onion (or chive)
   bacon rashers, finely   grated or finely chopped
   chopped)

Lightly fry bacon and add onion, stirring gently. Add half the quantity of water (or coconut milk) and bring to the boil. Stir remaining water into cornmeal; add salt and pour into boiling water, stirring all the time to prevent lumping. Reduce heat and simmer until it is thick and smooth, stirring occasionally. Turn into a well buttered basin or mould. Leftover cou-cou can be sliced and fried or grilled. Okras may be added to this dish. The term cou-cou means a cooked side dish. This can be made with other vegetables like grated cassava or breadfruit.

The breadfruit is another favourite food and can be used in many recipes in place of potato. It is boiled, steamed, roasted or baked, and has a pleasant, subtle flavour.

A 'one-pot' is often the main meal in local homes; for example a pilau of stewed beef or chicken cooked with rice; a fish broth with vegetables and dumplings; a hearty soup of pigeon peas (a tropical legume, the pods growing on a shrub rather than a vine) cooked with salt beef and dumplings; or perhaps an oil down for which the recipe is given below.

Oil down

8 oz (225 g) [$\frac{1}{2}$ lb] salt meat   1 sprig native celery
   (beef or pork)   1 sprig each thyme and
1 large full breadfruit   parsley
2 pints (1 l) [5 cups] coconut   1 teaspoon salt
   milk   1 tablespoon curry powder or
1 hot green pepper   1 oz (25 g) [2 T] saffron
1 chive

Cut up meat into one-inch pieces. Soak for about half an hour. Meanwhile prepare coconut milk. Grate three large dry coconuts.

Pour on 2 pints of boiling water. Let stand until cool, then squeeze out milk. Peel and core breadfruit and cut into six or eight wedges. Cut up vegetables. Place meat in a heavy pot. Arrange breadfruit and vegetables on top, sprinkle on seasonings, salt, then coconut milk. Cover and bring to the boil. Add saffron (or curry powder) and simmer until meat is tender and the liquid absorbed. The oil from the coconut will be seen around the breadfruit. Serve hot.

Dasheen leaves (callaloo) can be added to this dish during cooking. It should be noted that coconut milk is not the water which is poured out of a mature green coconut. The milk is a creamy substance squeezed out of the grated meat with the help of some milk or water. If allowed to settle, this will separate, and the cream can then be skimmed off, sugar added, and used as a topping for desserts.

Christophene is a large ovoid-shaped pale green vegetable. This can be thinly peeled and cored, then sliced raw into salads, served with dips as an appetiser or cocktail snack, or lightly cooked and served with melted butter or a cheese sauce.

To end the meal, what about a choice of dessert?

When in season, mangoes are very much in demand, and the juice is often just sucked right out of the skin. It is a tasty addition to a fruit salad, or it can be served in a more fancy style.

Mango mousse

Ceylon mangoes are best as there are no strings. Any other mangoes used will have to be sieved after liquidising.

$1\frac{1}{4}$ cups mango pulp
Juice of 1 lime
2 teaspoons gelatine

8 oz (225 g) [1 cup] sugar
$\frac{1}{2}$ pint (300 ml) [$1\frac{1}{4}$ cups] evaporated milk, chilled

Soften gelatine in 2 tbsps water. Measure mango pulp and sugar and stir over gentle heat until sugar is dissolved. Add softened gelatine and lime juice. Chill until thick enough to mound slightly. Whip evaporated milk until thick. Fold in the mango mixture and pour into serving glasses or mould to set. Serves 6.

The French cashew is a small pear-shaped fruit which can be used in the place of apples in most recipes. The thin, red skin hides the pure white flesh which is crisp and tasty when eaten raw. It is a nice addition to fruit or vegetable salads, or as a dessert.

French cashew crumble

6 large French cashews
1 teaspoon cinnamon
2 oz (50 g) [$\frac{1}{4}$ cup] sugar

2 oz (50 g) [$\frac{1}{4}$ cup] butter or
margarine
8 oz (225 g) [1 cup] oatmeal

Slice the fruit thinly into a shallow greased baking dish. Sprinkle with half the sugar, mixed with cinnamon. Mix oatmeal with the other half of sugar. Melt butter, stir in oatmeal and sugar and mix thoroughly. Sprinkle over fruit. Bake in a hot oven about 450°F for 30 minutes until topping is crisp and browned. Serve hot or cold, with or without a custard sauce.

A small amount of coffee is grown and sold locally and can be percolated in the normal way.
To complete the repast we offer a local liqueur.

Sorrel liqueur

1 lb (450 g) [1 lb] sorrel
1 lb (450 g) [1 lb] sugar

1 pint ($\frac{1}{2}$ l) [$2\frac{1}{2}$ cups] rum
or brandy
1 teaspoon Angostura bitters

Cut off fruit close to the crown and discard the crown and seed. Place the fruit in a jar. Press down tightly. Add sugar and bitters. Cover with rum and let soak for about two days. Strain and bottle. Bon Appétit!

|17|
Useful information and addresses

English is the main language spoken on the island.

Climate – Tropical. Average annual shade temperature 85°F (30°C)
Dry season – January to May
Wet season – June to December

Clothing – Light summer clothing is worn year-round. No Grenadian
can afford to be dressed by a couturier, but in town we wear
simple, tasteful jeans, shorts and light clothing. Bikinis and 'short
little shorts' are kept for the beach. We would be happy if
visitors to our islands followed our example.
Entertainment is usually informal and decent sportswear is
acceptable.

Medical and dental facilities are easily available.

Our water is quite safe for drinking.

Electricity rating at 220/240 volts, 50 cycles AC.

The Eastern Caribbean Dollar is the official monetary unit. One
United States dollar is fixed at EC$2.70. US Money Orders and
travellers' cheques are exchanged at a slightly lower rate. The
rates at which all other currencies are exchanged fluctuate daily.
Up-to-date rates can be obtained from any bank. US notes are
exchanged at EC$2.67 to the US dollar.

Communications – Cable & Wireless Grenada Ltd offers telex and
telegraphic services as well as fax. A cellular telephone service is
also available. Their offices are open Monday to Friday from
7.30 a.m. to 6.00 p.m.; Saturday from 7.30 a.m. to 1.00 p.m. and
on Sundays and public holidays from 10.00 a.m. to 12.00 noon.

Car rentals, sightseeing tours and yacht rentals and charters are easily
arranged through hotels, guest houses, travel agencies or the

Looking over the harbour at the Bay Town (SINCLAIR)

Board of Tourism. Please remember that we drive on the left-hand side of the road.

Business hours – most stores are open every weekday from 8.00 a.m. to 4.00 p.m. Some close for lunch from 11.45 a.m. to 1.00 p.m. On Saturdays, the hours are from 8.00 a.m. to 12.00 noon.

The Post Office is open daily from 8.00 a.m. to 4.00 p.m. Closed for lunch (with the exception of the stamps counter) from 11.45 a.m. to 1.00 p.m. Also closed on Saturdays and Sundays.

Hairdressers normally operate between 8.00 a.m. and 4.00 p.m.

Banks are open generally from 8.00 a.m. to 3.00 p.m. Monday to Thursday, Fridays from 8.00 a.m. to 5.00 p.m.

All major credit cards are accepted at leading hotels, stores and banks. It is wiser to have cash or travellers' cheques when shopping at the smaller boutiques.

Grenada International Travel Service (GITS) in Church Street is the American Express representative on the island.

Duty-free shopping is available at the airport and at some shops on the Carenage. Cameras, watches, French perfumes, china, jewellery and liquor are all offered there.

The airport departure tax is EC$50.00

Travel agencies:

Astral Travel & Tours
The Carenage, St George's
Tel: 440-5127/5180
Fax: 440-5466

Carin Travel Service
Grand Anse, St George's
Tel: 444-4363/4364
Fax: 444-4560

Grenada International Travel
Service
Church St, St George's
Tel: 440-2945
Grand Anse, St George's
Tel: 444-3373
Carriacou
Tel: 443-6666
Fax: 440-4091

Huggins Travel Service
The Carenage, St George's
Tel: 440-2090/2514

Joy's Travel Service
The Carenage, St George's
Tel: 440-5720/5721

Kayams Travel & Tours
International
The Carenage, St George's
Tel: 440-2312

MAPS Travel Services
Gladstone Rd, Grenville
St Andrew's
Tel: 442-7064
Fax: 442-7021

M & C Travel Agency
The Carenage, St George's
Tel: 440-2371/1475
Fax: 440-6653

Prime Travel Inc.
Lauriston Airport, Carriacou
Tel: 443-6677

Ramdhanny's Travel Service
Grenville, St Andrew's,
Tel: 440-7929; 442-7726
Main Street, Sauteurs,
Tel: 442-9417

Regency Travel Service
Halifax St, St George's
Tel: 440-1827

United Travel Agency
Young St, St George's
Tel: 440-0118/0119
Fax: 440-6310

Useful addresses

The Grenada Board of Tourism
Burns Point
P.O. Box 293,
St George's, Grenada, West Indies
Tel: 473-2279/440-2001
Email gbt@caribsurf.com
www.grenadagrenadines.com

Government of Grenada overseas offices

Grenada Board of Tourism:

USA
317 Madison Avenue, Suite 1522,
New York, NY 10017,
USA
Tel: 212 687 9554
Toll Free: 800-927 9554
Fax: 212 573 9731
Email: noel@rfcp.com

United Kingdom
1 Battersea Church Road,
London SW11 3LY,
United Kingdom
Tel: 020 7771 7016
Fax: 020 7771 7181
Email: grenada@cibgroup.co.uk

Canada
439 University Ave. Suite 920,
Toronto, Ontario M5G 1Y8,
Canada
Tel: 416 595 1339
Fax: 416 595 8279
Email:
tourism@grenadaconsulate.com

Germany
Uhlandstrasse 30,
D-53340 Meckenheim,
Germany
Tel: 02225 947 507
Fax: 02225 947 508
Email: RMTours87@aol.com

Austria
Discover the World,
Stephansplatz 6/3/7,
A-1010 Wien
Tel: 01 512 86 86 40
Fax: 01 512 86 86 60
Email:
Discover_vie@compuserve.com